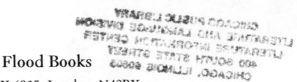

Flood Books

P.O. BOX 6835, London, N42BY

First published 1995 except, Looking at You (revived) Again,
first published 1989

Design Laurence Muspratt

ISBN *0 9525445 0 4*

Printed & Bound by: Deluxe Printers Tel: 0181-965-1771

errata:

p40	you'll back	*reads*	you'll look back
p43	you shoulders?	*reads*	your shoulders?
p47	about out it	*reads*	about it
p54	and antimassock	*reads*	an antimacassock
p64	big young	*reads*	bit young
p71	your find words	*reads*	your fine words
p78	for hear	*reads*	for fear
p85	away form me	*reads*	away from me
p96	it makes me feel ill	*reads*	
	it makes me feel..		
p111	Strength in you yet help me	*reads*	
	Strength in you yet to help me		
p144	But if got the chance	*reads*	
	But if I got the chance		
p152	Course they course they do	*reads*	
	Course they do course they do		
p155	**uncle** ...You are a cunt	*reads*	
	aunty ...You are a cunt		
back cover	La Liberation	*reads*	Liberation

*   *   *

Contents:

First performed at Royal Court Theatre Upstairs in July 1993

The Terrible Voice Of Satan

A MAN AT A URINAL

man   This is the story of Tom Doheny, a figure in popular lore. some fools say he was the devil, some say just a plain honest Irish man. Some say he was two fellas, some three, others that the trinity was divisible, or that he was a boat load of adventurers, others that Tom Doheny was the name of the boat itself, but then in that case who was it came on the boat, and where did they put ashore and inevitably what were their names and what the name of their god? This last is answered, albeit partially, by the old saying; if you want to know a people's god, look at their devil. Your lordships I give you Tom Doheny, hero, heroine, vessel of all our hopes, traitor, thief, braggart

LIGHTS OUT

Hey! Ah my shoes!

       ★   ★   ★

TOM DOHENY, A MAN WITH ENORMOUS BOOTS WHEELS A WHEELBARROW. INSIDE IT IS A SKINNY WHITE HAIRED OLD WOMAN, HIS MOTHER. OUT IN FRONT, A TIRED OLD MAN IN A FILTHY GREY SUIT IS WALKING AS IF LEADING THE PARTY, BUT THOUGH HE MANIPULATES HIS CANE BOLDLY HE IS LOST

ma   Get some speed up Tom, we'll be perished by the cold

tom   Why don't you give us a song as we go

ma   I will not. I have sung my throat to ribbons over the Christmas festivities, I'm voiceless

tom   A great quality in a mother

ma   Never you mind your qualities get some elbow into it. Oh why did we have to come on the boat, why didn't we fly over like decent people?

da   The boat's fine

ma   Gee you're earthbound if ever a man was. Don't be earthbound like your father son

da   You trample me into the mud with every word and then you expect me to rise like a phoenix from the pile of insults you heap on top of me. I'd just as soon die now and be done with it. Stop off now at this

	cemetery on the left son and save yourself the trouble later on
ma	Go on but who'll dig your grave for you? I can't see you doing it. No, I guess you're stuck in the land of the living, too bone idle to die
da	Bone idle is it? There's more calluses on these hands than on your face even

A BEAUTIFUL WOMAN WALKS PAST, EFFORTLESSLY OVERTAKING THE WHEEL-
BARROW AND STRIDING OFF AHEAD

ma	What was that?
tom	My future wife
ma	Ha listen to him. Good luck to you son
tom	Wait there (HE CLOMPS OFF IN HASTE HINDERED BY HIS GIANT SHOES)
ma	Your son's gone to make a fool of himself, running after that mare with great long legs on her and the devil's own petticoat or what was she wearing?
da	What do I care? This is all a dream. I'm still at home with the piggies

ENTER A PRIEST IN A LONG BLACK CASSOCK

priest	No, wrong. You're in God's house
ma	Ah you frightened me father! But this is the edge of a turnip field, a beach beside the sea
priest	You are a disgrace to the Irish race! Don't you realise this is a cathedral? You are inside one of the biggest churches in the world
da	Jeez, they make 'em big here
priest	That's right fella, you'd better get used to it. Quick now, down on your knees and beg forgiveness before anyone sees you, come on, come on

HE FORCES THEM TO KNEEL IN THE MUD

THE WIND BEGINS TO HOWL

Don't you know the devil stalks these cliffs looking for souls such as yours. He's around here now. Pray for God's sake!

THE OLD COUPLE CLASP THEIR HANDS TOGETHER IN PRAYER AND START MUMBLING

THUNDER AND LIGHTNING

He'll make monsters of us all, he'll creep up on you and climb up on your shoulder and be there whispering and whispering until you can't bear it. Because do you know what he does, do you know what Satan does?

ma & da	(IN TERROR) No father, what does he do?
priest	He speaks the truth!

THUNDER AND LIGHTNING

ma & da	Argh! (THEY COWER IN HORROR AT THESE WORDS)
priest	Pray! Go on in Christ's name pray!
da	Will you pray with us father?
priest	Don't be ridiculous man! I've got to keep the look out. (HE TUGS AT HIS HAIR IN DESPAIR AS THEY FALL TO PRAYING)

TOM COMES BACK MAKING THEM ALL JUMP

priest	This is him! Get behind me Satan!
tom	What's going on?
da	The good father has advised we should pray son, where have you been?
tom	Aah, I've been and picked these seven wild flowers with that young lady. And now I will sleep with them under my pillow and with any luck I'll dream of the one I am to marry. She'll do the same with the seven she picked - what a great girl - Goodnight

HE TAKES OFF ONE OF HIS ENORMOUS BOOTS AND PLACES THE SEVEN FLOWERS UNDER IT AND RESTS HIS HEAD UPON IT AS A PILLOW

priest	(CROSSES HIMSELF) Good night good people, God bless and protect you, snuff the candles on your way out

★   ★   ★

TOM SLEEPS. A DARK SHAPE APPEARS AT HIS FEET DANCING IN THE DARKNESS, OCCASIONALLY STRUCK BY LIGHTNING AS IT DOES SO

magic bird	Ah Tom, Tom Doheny, so you're here after all at last. Haven't I been waiting for you?
tom	Who are you?
magic bird	I am the Magic Bird that dances at your feet, I'm the girl you are to marry, I'm your tombstone too, they call it a headstone but what do they know? The stone is always at your feet boy. Now tell me, what will you do here?
tom	Don't ask me, I'm here on account of my ambitious mother
magic bird	Parents. You don't need them now! Send them off to sea!
tom	No-one needs them now poor loves, thinking of them brings a lump to my throat
magic bird	A lump? Hope it's not cancer. I hear it can be painful
	GRABS HIS KNEE BOISTEROUSLY
tom	Argh! What's that?
magic bird	That's the old knee-grab; a playful tool to see if you're awake. Come on now take me to Holy Joe's I want to pray
tom	We're already there sir
magic bird	Alright then, on your knees. Now what will you ask His Reverence for? A new job or a new life altogether? Come on make your mind up, I haven't got all day
tom	This must be a dream
magic bird	If you don't like it you can leave, I'm not here to dance favour on you laddoe
tom	Stop jumping about, sit still!
magic bird	I can't, I have to keep moving or I'll be struck by lightning. It's the curse His Lordship put on me when I told him what I thought of him
tom	Did you? Did you do that?
magic bird	Of course I did, what do you take me for?
tom	That's what I'd like to be like, bold and frightening
magic bird	You already are, I'd heard of you

10

tom	Had you?
magic bird	(SUDDENLY AGGRESSIVE) Can't find anyone to blame!? Well then, you'll have to wind your neck in!
tom	What?

★   ★   ★

TOM CATCHES UP WITH THE PRIEST

tom	Father, Father, wait!
priest	So its you
tom	I'm not bad father, I swear to you
priest	I know. I know it. Forgive me
tom	I'm just a simple working man
priest	The problem is my boy that I've gone mad. I have delusions. I'd seek a cure apart from the fact that I rather like them
tom	Actually I came to ask you a favour
priest	Good lad. I could tell by your blackened teeth you were a man to be trusted. What can I do for you?
tom	Marry me to that long legged girl I was with tonight
priest	If you can find her, I'll do it for you. Though strictly I'm enjoying an early retirement on account of my doctrinal hesitations
tom	Can't those be overcome, with study father?
priest	Isn't that precisely what my Lord Bishop said to me yesterday. I have a little grog under my cot if you care to follow me home. You could perhaps help me out of my anathema
	THEY SET OFF
	Oh, what about your aged parents?
tom	I left them parked in the swamp, they seemed happy enough with it
priest	Bless them

★   ★   ★

TOM DOHENY'S HEAD APPEARS FROM A HOLE AT GROUND LEVEL. ALONG COMES A PAIR OF BOOTS AND A PAIR OF LADIES SHOES

nellie   What's that?

man   A navvies head. Otherwise known as the devils football

THE HEAD STARTS DIGGING

nellie   What are you doing?

tom   Digging missus

nellie   He's digging. He's ever so strong. What muscles!

a voice some way off   Come up out of that hole and help us Tom Doheny

THE HEAD SMILES TO ITSELF

man   You bloody navvy, what do you have to keep digging holes for? Don't you know people fall into them and hurt themselves! For Christ's sake soon the whole world will a paddy's hole

tom   I know what you mean and all health to your worship. I'd stop right now if it weren't for one thing

nellie   What's that?

tom   My poor dead mummy and daddy

A PAIR OF BLACK BROGUES UNDER A CASSOCK APPEARS ALONGSIDE THE BOOTS AND SHOES

priest   Nonsense Tom, they're right as rain, sure there's nothing the matter with them at all. Hardly what you'd call dead at any rate

tom   Alright so. It's for my friend the priest. It's for his sake alone that I am digging

priest   It's true. It's all on account of me

nellie   I'm in love, I'm in love with the Navvies head. What a wonderful man!

tom   Actually as it happens I'm not just a labouring man, I've many talents to benefit the world. I'm a doctor and, and a poet -

nellie   What poems have you written?

tom   None to date. Travelling is my first love

nellie   Where have you been?

tom	Across the Irish Sea. Twice
nellie	Twice? But you're in England. What was your original point of departure?
tom	Well dammit that's peculiar
nellie	Alright help him up, he's a genius. We'll set him on the road to riches
priest	Really no, I'd leave him there
nellie	No I can't. His little head looks so sorrowful at shoe level
tom	I like the idea of a new job Dan, it'd be an awful boost. And think of all the fun we'd have if I got rich
priest	I'll not be having fun with you Tom Doheny!
tom	The reverend father is embarrassed on account of all the evenings he and I passed the jar to and fro between us, the old tongue loosens, he's said some things I suppose he'd rather I didn't repeat
priest	In the name of God Tom I'm a man like any other
tom	I'm not holding it against you Dan
priest	He's a terrible one for the ladies as well, you can't trust him
nellie	Give us your hands Tom. Come on father help me

THEY ALL REACH DOWN AND PULL. THEY TUMBLE INTO THE HOLE, BOOTS, SHOES AND BROGUES

LIGHTS UP. A GIRL ON A BICYCLE, DRESSED IN WHITE RIDES PAST

LIGHTS DOWN

BICYCLE AND RIDER CLATTER DOWN INTO THE HOLE IN THE DARK

★　　★　　★

TOM DOHENY AND AN ELDERLY FRIEND

tom	So anyway I went into the hospital in an old white coat and started off with a few experiments of my own and what do you know? I'd discovered 17 real important cures
friend	There's the true luck of the Irish for you
tom	It all came from nowhere. My head was buzzing with inventions and marvels of all kinds. I pick up a pen and a beautiful poem

	appears. I whistle in the bath tub and I end up constructing cherubic melodies
friend	Here's my hand on that. I always said you were a great lad, a real success. Good boy! Good lad!
tom	But here's the real crux
friend	What? What is it?
tom	I discovered it was all worthless
friend	What? Worthless? A mistake surely
tom	Dross
friend	All your discoveries, your love songs?
tom	All of it
friend	The injections for little babies?
tom	Nothing at all. Worse than nothing
friend	I'm sorry to hear that. Whatever brought you to this conclusion?
tom	I have found their replacement, an inheritor
friend	A replacement? What can it be?
tom	I have discovered it
friend	What kind of thing is it?
tom	It is, the Magic Bird
friend	A bird?
tom	The cure of all ills upon us currently
friend	What was it you called this thing?
tom	The Magic Bird

★　　★　　★

THE TWO LOVERS ON A SANDY BEACH TOGETHER

tom	..and then there's my inheritance from my parents (CROSSES HIMSELF) God preserve them from all harm
nellie	Are they rich? They appeared destitute
tom	They are modest people. Beneath their indigent exteriors are hidden great stores of physical and spiritual wealth. They are like

two turtle doves whispering to each other all day

nellie (SHE SECRETLY CUTS HER FOOT WITH A BROKEN GLASS) That must be a great inspiration to you

tom It is yes. Don't you worry about me Captain because I'm a great believer in romance

nellie Oh so am I, so am I!

tom We'll be great together

nellie Oh Tom ...

tom Yes darlin'?

nellie I've hurt my foot

★   ★   ★

TOM DOHENY AND HIS MATES, LABOURERS

tom Yes boys I think I'll settle down

mates No, No!

tom Yes lads the time has come to lay down my fiddle, take off my boots and drain the last jar. After all I've a good woman waiting for me

liam But many others besides, don't forget them, bless their poor wayward hearts, the wild flowers of the wayside, condemned to blow forever, plagued by flies and the tinkers snout

tom Enough boys. I can't bear any more! Alright I'll come out one more time with ye. We'll drink a toast; To England that has made itself my home and raised me to great heights of fame

rory But don't forget-

tom -Ireland, the wild flower of the wayside

finn Where'll we go?

tom Up to Camden, then beyond to Archway and beyant..

liam What'll we do there?

tom We'll strip down to our woollies and dance with the plump girls of the North

rory And the lean colleens of the South

liam	Swing from infernal Archway Tower - and balance walk the rails of Suicide Bridge
tom & all	Off we go!

THEY GO

TOM STAYS BEHIND, THE GIRL ON THE BIKE CYCLES ROUND HIM. HE SMILES AT HER. SHE STOPS ALONGSIDE HIM. THE MOON APPEARS, SWITCHES ON LIKE A LAMP. A NIGHTINGALE SINGS A SUDDEN SONG

☆   ☆   ☆

TOM AND HIS MATES, AT THE DOG END OF THE EVENING, THE DAWN

liam	Hello there Tom
tom	Lads!
rory	What became of you?
tom	Oh! One of them wild flowers of the wayside turned up and I was indisposed to join you on your hedgerow rambles
liam	He's laughing at us is he?
finn	Is he? Are you laughing at us Tom?
liam	Is that it Hah?
rory	You've some strange English habits Tom
tom	Is that it? Well then lads, yes I am laughing at you
liam	Another wise crack and you'll be laughing with a cracked lip
tom	But lads I had a great adventure. Surely you don't think I should pass up on that to hold hands with you lot?
rory	He's too good for us
finn	You could have introduced us
liam	No, we're as common as dirt
rory	Didn't she have any friends?
tom	Fortunately not if my so-called friends are anything to go by
rory	You'll get along fine Tom
finn	Yes, you'll be a great scholar
liam	I reckon he'll end up an Englishman so he will

rory	Only don't count on our support when you're running for President of America
tom	Thanks lads for this
finn	You'd best go back to your film producers and your cardinals now Doheny
tom	I will, thanks
rory	Go back to your English virgins, if you can find them
finn	Yeah and all your literate friends
liam	All the nobs, go on back to them and see if they're the gullible crowd you took us for
tom	Oh I'm sure they are lads don't worry

★   ★   ★

TOM DOHENY WHEELS HIS WIFE ALONG IN A WHEELBARROW

nellie	I suppose I must be a great disappointment to you
tom	Not at all
nellie	I bet you're thinking; "I wouldn't have married her if I'd known I would end up wheeling her about, its not a nursemaid I wanted to be"
tom	You're quite wrong. I hadn't really noticed
nellie	I catch you looking at me. Don't you think I know I'm holding you back. You could be out somewhere with a healthy lass having a world of fun
tom	We have fun sometimes the two of us
nellie	You don't call this fun do you?
tom	Well it might be if you'd only stop moaning
nellie	Always that word of criticism
tom	I only said -
nellie	You criticise until there is nothing left of a person. You take away even their right to be wrong. In fact if it weren't for your constant scrutiny I wouldn't perhaps be like this. Have you thought of that?
tom	No I've never thought of that

nellie	I remember the day, it was a week ago now, our wedding day, that you first complained about my limp
tom	I wasn't complaining on my behalf
nellie	Don't tell me you were proud to have your new wife staggering as if three parts drunk. I've seen you watching those girls go past with their big strides
tom	Why don't you walk then?
nellie	I've lost all confidence. Every time I fell over I felt your eyes burning into me
tom	Then for God's sake get up and walk and I'll turn my back. Or walk off so I won't find you
nellie	I can't! Look! (SHE THROWS HERSELF OUT FROM THE WHEELBARROW)
tom	You didn't even try
nellie	I can't try, that's just it. I tried to try but something stopped me
tom	Then I don't know what I can do
nellie	I'll keep trying to try
tom	How will I know when you are making that particular effort?
nellie	You'll feel a tremor in the barrow. You must have noticed?
tom	Yes, a slight tremor, rarely
nellie	That's the signal
tom	The tremor serves unaccountably to remind me of the passing of time. It's like a knell. Can't we do without it?
nellie	Only if I stop trying. And you want me to try don't you. Otherwise you would feel bound to me like this for ever. Then the absence of a tremor would also be a knell, the difference being that it would be constant. A constant *absence* of tremor. You choose
tom	I can't. Everything is a reminder. Death itself is reduced to the role of a reminder
nellie	You mean I am worse than a fatal disease?
tom	Yes you are like a disease that is not fatal and therefore has no end
nellie	I'm surprised to find this cantankerous side in you. When I saw you

in your hole I thought you would be above small differences. I noticed the way you served your poor parents digging your father's grave at his command regardless of his obstinate good health, a dutiful son I thought. A firm hand on a shovel if one was needed. Instead I find you an egotist. After all, I have my good days when I am up and running, then my legs are like anyone else's, better in fact. (HITCHES UP HER DRESS AND SHOWS HIM HER GARTERED THIGH) If there's company. I don't hear you praising me for that

tom   I'm always praising you. I praise you so much I nearly believe it myself

nellie   What a bitter man, and what a bully

★   ★   ★

TOM STANDS WEARILY. THE PRIEST APPROACHES

priest   I've bad news for you Tom

tom   Well don't be shy with it nothing could bring me down now, I'm on the crest of a wave

priest   Your parents have drowned

tom   Both of them? Jeez, it never rains

priest   Terrible when you consider it was you sent them on a luxury cruise from the proceeds of your..

tom   I have returned them to the sea whence they came

★   ★   ★

A GRAVEYARD ON TOP OF A HILL

priest   Look at the view there, isn't it marvellous!

tom   Mercy we are high up, I didn't notice the climb

A FUNERAL CORTEGE ARRIVES ALONGSIDE THEM

priest   Well, Tom, let's get on and bury them shall we?

tom   They came and whispered into my ear

priest   Who whispered in your ear?

tom   The laddoes left a sly bottle of whiskey, just left it on the side there as they went out

priest	There's a good crowd anyway
tom	I find the bitterness of death only partially alleviated by the joviality of a funeral

THE PRIEST READS FROM HIS BOOK IN LATIN

sexton	You know there's nothing in dem boxes
his gormless pal	Nothing at all?
sexton	Not a bone. Sure the two of them were lost at sea
gormless pal	Diabolical luck

TOM'S WIFE NELLIE STRUGGLES ALONG, DRUNK, NOT IN MOURNING

nellie	Father forgive me I know I shouldn't be here like this but maybe you can help me. I need something, something is missing, there always has been but what is it?
priest	I'm sure I don't know
nellie	Oh but I do! Guidance father. I need someone to tell me right from wrong
priest	Well I'm the last person to come to for that
nellie	Father you must help me I'm past despair
priest	Not my department girlie, I'm likely more depressed than you are. Now Tom Doheny's more your man..
nellie	Tom? Hah ha. He's no help at all. It's Tom Doheny this, Tom Doheny that, everyone has such high regard for his talents but what is he? A navvy. Such rumours spread, he's a doctor, a businessman, a politician, a real solver of problems. Well I'll tell you about Tom Doheny; He has another woman
priest	Is this true Tom?
tom	I wouldn't say 'have'
priest	What sophistry is that? Have you or haven't you?
nellie	He's *had* her is what he means to say
priest	Please Nellie I know Tom wouldn't boast in that vulgar way about what shall we call them, his amorous adventures
tom	Quite right

nellie	I've seen him riding on the back of her bicycle in the moonlight when he ought to have been with me
priest	I take a dim view Tom
tom	Christ Father, she was a perfect stranger. I was attending to her inner tube
priest	Well, if that's true my son-
nellie	What? Astride her panniers? That's a damned unusual position
tom	The unusual positions are sometimes the best
nellie	(RECOILS IN HORROR) You see! And this is the man you'd have me take as my moral guide
priest	But what kind of ethical certainties do you require? I think you're setting your demands too high. After all you are only an ordinary woman, it's not as if you are about to scale any peaks of virtue or, I hope, plough any troughs of malcreancy
nellie	You're wrong. My inner landscape has to be seen to be believed
priest	Take your wife in hand Tom. Give her what she needs. You must have picked her for this interesting side of her nature
tom	Yes indeed she looked at me with such penetration I was bewitched
priest	There you are then
tom	But I had mistaken it. She was in fact gawping in utter confusion. Am I right?
nellie	True father. I am not of this world. It's a mystery to me. It's all in a foreign language. They speak to me of many things but my ears are searching only for words of sympathy, I am deaf to all else
priest	Then my son you are a fool and have only yourself to blame
nellie	What should I do? (TURNS TO TOM) Those seven flowers, you have trampled them
tom	And you?
nellie	Should I offer hope? Where shall I go? Away? Alone?
tom	No, you'd only return

★　　★　　★

ON A HILLTOP, A DRY LITTLE MAN IN AN ANORAK

A WILD WIND BLOWS THEN FADES AWAY

THE WIND COMES AGAIN

dry man	So, you've come to the point in your life when you'd like some power
tom	Right! I'm past crucifying age, now I want what's mine
dry man	Then rise up and take it
tom	But.. my energies are beginning to flag
dry man	That's tough luck indeed..
tom	What wickedness is it forces a young man to spend his best energies kicking his heels and then be called upon to raise the battle cry just when his life is crumbling about his ears
dry man	You'd best put a brave face on it because your difficulties will only grow from now on
tom	I'm in the grips of a terrible fear, I'm scared of the dark but I can't stand the light, I can't bear company but I can't be alone, I can neither travel nor stay put..
dry man	Try to be a man for God's sake!
tom	All my energies are spent watching my loved ones suffer and myself suffer at their hands
dry man	I'll give you hope
tom	I want shelter. I look at you and I see a desert. I don't want it
dry man	Oh I know you're hankering for fruit, soft pears in the sunshine, a peaceful garden and a lake, but what's beckoning there is nothing but death itself. You must deny it and follow me instead; my dry skin, my stiff bones, I smell of pickled fish and remind you of lonely men, the world of handshakes and barren evenings. - Life laddie, life! A lonely activity on a nondescript road
tom	Leading where?
dry man	Away, always away
tom	(LOOKS AT HIM IN HORROR)

dry man	You're not with any of your bloody women now! You can feel disgusted all you want

THE MAN FALLS DOWN IN A FIT. TOM WATCHES, NOT KNOWING WHAT TO DO

dry man	Aren't you going to help me?
tom	What can I do? You're mad. Look where your tough talking has got you. You're a cripple, a piss-soaked cripple
dry man	A cripple is it? Don't let this fool you!

MORE CONVULSING

What are you afraid of? You'll end up like this perhaps?

Come here (HIS GRIP IS IRON STRONG) Taste this

HE FORCES TOM TO LICK THE CORNERS OF HIS MOUTH WHERE THE FROTH HAS FORMED

tom	Urgh! It's salt. Leave me alone!
dry man	Salt you see, not foam, but salt. Salt, life!
tom	I'm so thirsty. Let go!
dry man	Why do you think Jesus was thirsty on the cross? Salt, salt! He was made to live a million salty lives in a few hours
tom	*No*! It doesn't have to be like this. Life is sweet and young and full of love and light!

★   ★   ★

THE DRY MAN IS REPLACED BY A PARTY GUEST

guest	So where are your friends and family now Tom? Eh? Not feeling lonesome are you? Come on back into the funeral party. It's all in your honour. Aren't you the one's made great advances in science and come up with the cures for all those diseases?
tom	It is, Sir
guest	Don't be modest with me now Tom. Medicine is an important art, no-one can deny that... Of course disease too is a great leveller isn't it? It's a part of life and in all fairness where would we be without it?

(TOM IS LOOKING ROUND)

	Are you looking for your wife Tom? Don't you worry about her now, come over and talk to the boys
mr coomey	...you tell me why you're not funny any more?
mr hackett	Because I can no longer summons up the arrogance to laugh at others and I'm damned if I'm going to laugh at myself
coomey	Ah Tom, Mr Hackett was telling me you have some interesting thoughts on recent political developments
tom	I wouldn't say that
hackett	We were just talking about our black friends, and the queers. Very problematic cases all in all
tom	Well it's obvious you must subject the innocent victim to a good beating inspired by your worst prejudices. That way you know what they're really up against
coomey	He's a real scream isn't he?
bubbles	The most foul-mouthed braggart that ever carried a hod
tom	I look inside at the commonplaces in my mind and I wonder how life about me goes on unharmed; the niggers and the queers, the bums and the jerks, I expect them all to tumble to pieces in the aura of my being. How I survive them and they me is a mystery
hackett	You sound like a jesuit. You are destined for greatness surely
tom	I have insured myself against greatness by marrying a donkey
	IN THE BACKGROUND HIS WIFE DRESSED IN BLACK TIGHTS AND A TOP HAT PERFORMS ROUTINE MAGIC TRICKS IN A MATTER OF FACT MANNER
bubbles	She seems drunk, is she drunk?
guest	That priest, the one with the paintings, don't you think you might have offended him with your remarks on his work? He's gone off leaving them all behind
tom	I said it to help him god damn him. I'll auction them. This one. Three hundred pounds!
coomey	Four. Five!
tom	I think I started too low
bubbles	Six!

tom	Stop Stop! I'm starting at a thousand
hackett	Your wife is taking her clothes off
tom	Let her
coomey	She's a wonderful woman by the looks of her. Great shoes
hackett	(TO COOMEY) Not short of sixpence I can promise you
coomey	Men friends?
hackett	Men friends, women friends, friends of all descriptions
coomey	Who is that blighter in the big coat?
hackett	So you are the one with this strange phoenix. But I have heard it was not your discovery alone
tom	Not my discovery?
hackett	You've been spotted out by the rubbish bins whispering in corners with a dried up old man who, it is said, was walking around with a very similar gadget 40, 50 years ago. How do you like that?
tom	I don't care for your speculations. You'll see nothing of this creature until it is already dead
hackett	Tell us, what does it do?
tom	Nothing at all. Except...
hackett	Yes?
tom	It speaks the truth
hackett	A likely story. Where is it, let's hear it
tom	As you should all know, truth is a shy virgin
coomey	I've tried Lao-tse, Kwang-tzu, Nietsche, Buber, Russell, Isiah Berlin, Isiah the prophet, Jung, Jesus, the I-Ching..
guest	You are drowning in a sea of wistfulness
coomey	No, I'm being eaten by the sharks of regret
bubbles	There they go with their metaphors
tom	Who'll give me fifteen hundred?
bubbles	I feel drawn towards logical expression
hackett	It must be old age creeping on. Senility
coomey	..punching walls, begging, pleading, stomping, shouting..

bubbles	(TO JULIE) Even the most useless person with no particular knowledge or talent - when they die and the contents of their heads are poured out, unexpected treasures will appear and you may say to their spirit "oh did you know that song? or remember that place?"
coomey	..crying, lying, dirty weekends, writing letters, making friends, losing friends, library books, suspender belts, headache pills, falling in love, and I've even written a letter to the Queen protesting about the state of her prisons. And where did it all get me?
hackett	Where?
coomey	Nowhere. Bloody nowhere
bubbles	(TO JULIE) At least our children needn't all be Americans. They might be Sudanese
hackett	At least then they'll be able to read
guest	So at last the nightnurse arrived and tended to my every need
bubbles	What a genius
coomey	(TO TOM) The major and minor poets, Irish, Jewish and downright English. I've tried sport, food, yoghurt, cigarettes, tea, cakes, stews, touching my toes, hot baths, sleep, toothbrushing, doctors, dentist, priest, watched the news, stayed at home, gone out, isolation, immolation, socialising, advertising, agoraphobia, claustrophobia, epilepsy, coke and pepsi, dark glasses, clean socks, buying plants, framing pictures -
bubbles	One of his eyelids was loose!
coomey	(TO TOM) Am I boring you?
bubbles	(TO GUEST) How is Louise?
guest	Mad as a hatter
hackett	My masturbation is a great source of jealousy to my wife. As well it ought to be
coomey	God I'm lonely
hackett	Ha! There was a time when I would have felt pity for you but nowadays everyone is lonely, everyone is upset, but ask them why they are upset and they can't tell you

julie	(TO BUBBLES) My reading? Mainly medieval history. And of course Eichendorf
hackett	Domestic life is difficult when an offer of tea is met with a glare of primal hatred
bubbles	(TO JULIE) No, don't write it at home, write it out here; stretched out on the sandy common
hackett	(TO COOMEY AND TOM) I'm telling you politics to me is like reproduction to a tart. An unnecessary evil to be avoided
bubbles	(TO JULIE) If I exaggerate it's only in the cause of truth
coomey	He'd make a lousy tart wouldn't you think?
tom	I don't know. (HE NOTICES NELLIE AND THE PRIEST)
coomey	He keeps his spiritual legs firmly crossed
bubbles	Look why don't you just tell me who you vote for
hackett	(TO JULIE) Do you think he wants you eh? He doesn't want you!
coomey	You complain about your wife but just imagine if there was only the Exodus, the untrue, and the One who didn't believe you?
guest	The one who didn't believe me? When she departed all truth went out of my life
hackett	Give me a drink in the name of Jesus
	IN THE BACKGROUND THE PRIEST AND NELLIE ARE DANCING FACING EACH OTHER, PELVICALLY
tom	Alright everyone time to go home, you're too drunk
bubbles	He's power mad
tom	Why do all the women in this room have such a strong vaginal odour?
bubbles	This is Julie. Did you know she can actually see your aura? She's here about the rainforests aren't you dear?
tom	Now Julie I'd guess you're the kind of girl's not wearing any knickers, am I right?
julie	I flew in this morning. I love airports don't you? They're so 1950s
coomey	I'm sorry but I find the whole thing embarrassing

guest	It would be alright if Tom weren't so obviously showing off

IN THE BACKGROUND TOM'S WIFE IS ASTRIDE THE PRIEST SHOUTING THE
SLOGAN "DEEP RED SEA, DEEP RED SEA" WHILE HE CONDUCTS HER

hackett	Is that the cuckolds anthem I hear?
coomey	His greatest admirer once
hackett	No more it seems

TOM RUSHES UP

tom   How dare you betray me in front of everyone with a critic

HE SLAPS HER CLUMSILY CATCHING HER FULL ON THE NOSE. INSTANTLY HER
FACE AND CLOTHES ARE COVERED IN BLOOD

bubbles   I should say it serves him right

coomey   (IN A SOUR MUMBLE) Critics. I wish I got paid for slandering my
betters

★   ★   ★

A PARTY GUEST LEADS TOM OUTSIDE INTO THE STREET, PULLING ON AN
ANORAK, HE IS THE DRY MAN

dry man   I'd say you need some air. (LEADS HIM OUT) So, the tragic balloon of
optimism has burst

tom   (WHO IS A BIT DRUNK) I'm too gentle and forgiving. There's nothing
like endless patience for provoking cruelty. Do you have a wife?

dry man   I do. The slut. She's living it up in gaol while I'm stuck out here

tom   You must miss her

dry man   I do, but I have another. Don't you?

tom   I certainly do thank Christ. Now she's awful nice to me. She orders
me to stay. 'I need you' she says! 'I can't!' I said 'I'm pledged to
another' and the door slammed in my face before I had time to step
back inside for I had decided to stay

dry man   What a laddoe! Not a thought for the consequences?

tom   Love learns no lessons

THE GIRL IN WHITE APPEARS RIDING HER BICYCLE

girl in white   I do laugh when I think of you at a bus stop with your erection,

	comparing one human being to another!
tom	Ha! And yet these are the ingredients and activities of love
girl in white	They are your only real achievements
tom	At least I've come of age and no longer care for secrecy
girl in white	Though secrecy still cares for you, hiding your one thought from another, doesn't it?
dry man	Ha, ha! Funny how when your marriage goes sour you can only keep alive your faith in love through adultery! Isn't that the irony of it!
tom	Don't ask me to leave her and go on believing in love. How would I love you then? Would I then desert you too if you became ill like her and made me unhappy?

SHE LUNGES AT HIM WITH A PENKNIFE, PLUNGING IT INTO HIS THIGH LEAVING IT THERE. SHE RIDES AWAY

| tom | She buried her penknife in my thigh, I kept it there to her shame. Only years later did I allow her to draw it out |

★   ★   ★

NELLIE HESITATING AT THE GATES OF MADNESS

SHE IS STEPPING TO AND FRO ACROSS THE THRESHOLD OF HER BEDROOM

nellie	..they say the worst thing about being in prison is that you become your own gaoler. They will come and open the doors one day and I shall simply stare across the threshold
tom	Yes, you say that and yet if I'm not mistaken you have the air of one with the travel fever..?
nellie	Yes, I'm going back to Germany. Here are my trunks, will you have them sent? You'll come with me later won't you?
tom	With you? But I'm ill, I, I meant to tell you
nellie	You didn't mention it
tom	You never gave me the chance. I have become a terror to myself, my body and soul are strangers to each other, my ears are blocked, my muscles are degenerating through under use
nellie	Pull yourself together. Do you have any strong rope? Tie them all

up, get them to the station, show your ticket, register the trunks for freight and that's it, done

tom   I'll never manage. No second thoughts?

nellie   None. Sanity beckons - you recoil in horror. Goodbye darling. I'm already looking forward to you coming. We'll unpack it all together. Think, how happy we'll be

★   ★   ★

AT HIS FRIEND THE PRIEST'S HOUSE

tom   She's gone. I can't begin to tell you the tortures I suffered at her hands

priest   Was she cruel?

tom   I like to say she was possessed

priest   Then why so afraid of her going?

tom   In a moment of weakness I resolved to take with me my sick wife of no comfort. Like the insecure child I take my inadequate mummy with me wherever I go

priest   But it's not you travelling, it's her

tom   So it is. Can you help me with these?

priest   No damn you

★   ★   ★

THE DRY MAN APPEARS AT HIS SIDE

dry man   So your best friend says you have no backbone?

tom   He curses me for my weakness to the same degree that he worshipped me for my strength. He's nursing his wounds

dry man   Never let idolaters be your friends. You must let them swear their allegiance, then run for it

tom   He was strangely lacking in loyalty I thought..

dry man   They idolise you so they can hate you, blame you for everything that is wrong with themselves. They seem to give you all power on earth but keep for themselves the sacred power of resentment

tom   You've a point there

dry man   They will gather together in your name and swear your destruction. And though you may sit at home trembling, afraid to leave your four walls, or you may crawl meekly from tree to tree along a quiet street and be saying to yourself, consoling yourself, saying

IN A QUIET STREET

tom   I will go and see my friend for I am truly in need of a friend

dry man   ..he will open the door snarling and say..

friend   What do you come here for? Do you think I'm at your beck and call? To be visited when you feel like it? No, I want to be alone. You weakling. So you can't sweat it out by yourself, you thought you'd use me. Well don't come back, I'll see you in a year. To think I used to admire you, you spider!

ALONE IN THE STREET

tom   So I did what I was told, and I did not go back even though the mound of suitcases on my floor tumbled perpetually up and down my stairs, left there by my wife for me to take to the station, the pile grew amid tangles of rope. Have you ever noticed the similarity between a trunk and a coffin?

And so heavy were they and so dizzy was I that I could not carry them and I went in sorrow to a certain person who opened her door and took me in her arms and fed me with blood from her broken heart. She carried my suitcases of her rival and buttoned my coat and said Goodbye Again, goodbye again, and all joy to her forever and ever and God forgive me for being loved

THE GIRL IN WHITE RIDES PAST ON HER BICYCLE AND WAVES "BYE"

dry man   That's a touching story Tom. And shall we see how the man who loves to love, pays back this loyalty?

tom   (MODESTLY) No, no for God's sake I don't want that

dry man   No go on, let's see it, because do you know what? I always find it so inspiring, as I'm sure she did, didn't she, bless her?

TOM, ALMOST A MAGICIAN, SPREADS HIS LARGE WINGS IN A PROTECTIVE SWEEP. WITH A MASTERFUL AIR HE CUES THE WIND OF A STORM

A CHILD, AGED SIX, TRAILS IN BEHIND HER MOTHER, THE GIRL IN WHITE

child   Mummy I feel funny again

THE MOTHER STOPS, IT'S HAPPENING AGAIN. THE CHILD GOES INTO AN EPILEPTIC TRANCE, HEAD TO ONE SIDE JERKING SLIGHTLY

TOM DOES BATTLE WITH THE DISEASE

tom   I know you, I know exactly what to do. I will be here awake until the onslaught is over. With my second sight and my intuition I can see the enemy ranged against her fair head, and with the force of my heart I am outwitting it!

HE STRETCHES OUT HIS HANDS AND GRINDS HIS JAWS

THE CHILD FALLS BACK

tom   I know exactly what to do

THE MOTHER GETS THE CHILD TO ITS FEET AND LEADS IT AWAY

tom   I know exactly what to do

child   Mummy..

tom   Yes, I feel my powers returning

dry man   Yes, you're a fine big man Tom Doheny. All your friends can rely on you, I can see that for sure

          ★   ★   ★

A STREET

A MAN WITH A RED FACE, IN A DINNER SUIT

tom   There, sit down on that wall and rest

dry man   I fell down young fella and hit my head. I might fall under a car. I've a pain in my chest and all down my spine. Sure I know I haven't long to live

tom   Have you been drinking?

dry man   Of course I've been drinking. Give me your little hand, oh God bless you its half of mine, you're just a little babbie. Feel that grip.

tom   Formidable

dry man	Don't worry I won't hurt you. Do you know why? Because you're Irish. If you'd been anybody else I would have taken your wrist, like this and done that, like this, and your arm'd be broken
tom	I think the ambulance is coming
dry man	Did you call an ambulance? You little blighter. I'm going to run away
tom	Do you know Tom Clancy, he's a Cork man
dry man	Shut up. I knew them all before you was even born. They want me you know, they need a good man with the dynamite, "only you can do it Tom Doheny" they said. Oh Jesus me chest! Pins and needles in my fingers too. Skin like bloody leather, I was out digging ditches in the Yemen you know
tom	Give me your hospital card, I'll show it to them when they come. Is that you? Fine moustache
dry man	Never mind the bloody moustache, that's me! Feel that grip!

AMBULANCE ARRIVES

★   ★   ★

A SAFE HOUSE

TOM HAS STOLEN THE DRY MAN'S IDENTITY. THREE MEN WITH BLACK JACKETS

tom	(HOLDS UP CARD) This is me, never mind the bloody moustache
one of the men	Only you can do it Tom Doheny...
tom	There's going to be some re-thinking done here. Pure social bloody engineering. I've always been a strong believer in revolution
cell leader	Take this, little man, and stop your blather (HANDS HIM A KALASHNIKOFF)

★   ★   ★

STREET CORNER. HIDING FROM AN ANGRY CROWD

cell leader	Well Tom Doheny, that was a great thing, your social bloody engineering. Everyone's bloody dead to a man
tom	He who takes up the sword sends other people's sons to die by the sword.

cell leader	And now their mammies are going to have your guts for garters for it, how d'ye like that?

A LYNCHING BAND OF MURDEROUS MOTHERS APPROACHES

★　　★　　★

TOM IS HANGING UPSIDE DOWN FROM A TREE

tom	They hanged me upside down from a tree. No-one fed or watered me, I gave up the ghost. My friends, my so-called friends never came after me and so I presume they wish me good riddance

NELLIE APPEARS ALONGSIDE WITH THE DRY MAN

tom	(TO NELLIE) And you! You see how you've poisoned everyone against me. (HE RAILS AGAINST HER BUT HIS VOICE FADES AWAY) You always make a point of ducking when I swing my arms but I'm the one who's black and blue with the beatings you've given me, lord when I think of myself tears well up in my eyes..
nellie	He hung there for nine days. Wonderful. Made the worms and the slugs his brothers and sisters, that is; let what's at the bottom come to the top and what's topmost.. ..fall out of his ears
tom	I see you're not short of company
nellie	Yes I met this man, he's a great friend of yours isn't he? Why did you never introduce me to him?
tom	(TRYING TO HANG WITH AS MUCH DIGNITY AS POSSIBLE) Well at first I wasn't sure I could trust him
nellie	Ah Tom...
tom	...and now, I'm not sure he can trust me
nellie	Your political shenanigans didn't turn out too good did they?
tom	Help me down from here now will ya?
nellie	Tom, you look like a fledgling fallen out of its nest. Is that what you meant by the magic bird?

★　　★　　★

COURTROOM. TOM IS IN THE DOCK DOING A PILE OF IRONING

tom	I find it difficult to believe that the God of love would involve us in this terrifying struggle against evil. I've learnt my lesson

prosecution	(INDIGNANT) But what about freedom of speech?
tom	Freedom of speech is the perogative of those on favourable terms with their publishers
	THE GALLERY CHEER AND HE WAVES BACK, PLEASED
tom	..but if the world were up in arms against my book I should withdraw it at once and serve them right!
gallery	*Boo!* No-one wants your rotten book anyway!
judge	You have no principles, get on with your ironing
tom	(HE RETORTS, BRAVING THE HECKLERS) The whole world is like a bad tempered hedgehog, bristling with principles. Take pacifism for example, vastly overrated! It should only be used as a last resort
gallery	Hooray!
prosecution	But what about the defenceless victim?
tom	Exactly. Who would begrudge him the chance of raising his knee into the groin of his attacker as he goes under? Who would even comment upon it, let alone say he had abandoned a principle
	LAUGHS FROM THE GALLERY. TOM LAUGHS COYLY IN REPLY
prosecution	So you would resist tyranny at least
tom	Hitler gave tyranny a very bad name
	THE CROWD IN THE GALLERY BOO. HE RANTS IN REPLY
tom	Now we have to stand up to them all, whatever the cost. Except the tyranny of hunger of course. It's the human face of the aggressor that attracts us, probably because he is our mirror image, like an angry dog we bark at it
	APPLAUSE
prosecution	You speak from an ignorance of history no doubt
	THE GALLERY LAUGH
tom	Just one mention of the word "history" and people are tossing babies into the air and shooting them
	DARK MURMURS FROM THE GALLERY
judge	Let's not talk of war. Your ironing smells, you need that new freshener

faintly from a lone voice in the gallery	Whatever happened to old Tom Doheny?
judge	I think you are a bit of a fascist
tom	I know you do but my suburban friends think I'm very left wing... you might say to yourself 'do I know this man?' and you look at him and - sorry what were we talking about?
prosecution	You were having evil thoughts of mass destruction
tom	I ask you, who has not? We lived in the shadow of the bomb and the consequent illiteracy for so long
gallery	Ha ha, listen to Tom the politician, look at the mouth on him, a mug of tea and he's anybody's man
tom	Death you see...
prosecution	Ah yes?
tom	Death. Not understanding about life, how can you understand death?
prosecution	M'lud, the man's an imbecile
tom	I .. submit, let the son be the son, the father the father, the minister the minister, the ruler the ruler
judge	(ASIDE TO THE PROSECUTION LAWYER) What are you doing?
prosecution lawyer	(SCRATCHING HIMSELF FRANTICALLY) I have scabies m'lud
tom	I've had a lot of bad luck in my life. A friend of my wife's writes poison pen letters saying I am the enemy of life
a quipper in the gallery	She wouldn't be far wrong there..
tom	- but only last year this same person was wanting the two of us in bed at the same time!
judge	(FASCINATED DESPITE HIMSELF) Did you do it?
tom	We both went round, but they made me do the washing up
prosecution	Bad luck indeed. (WINKS TO THE JURY) You didn't follow them to bed after your domestic duties were done?
tom	Are you joking? They went off at eight o'clock, I never sleep before dawn. I need to see confirmed the promise of rebirth before I

	commit myself to the little death which is sleep
prosecution	You're afraid of the dark?
tom	Who would trust the one who waves the flag of evil?
prosecution	You're hemming yourself in there
tom	I know all about that
prosecution	You find blamelessness in your lethargy?
tom	The intelligence of your questioning is rare
prosecution	Your self disgust is an armoury against unpleasant surprises
tom	Don't overdo it professor
prosecution	What would you say is your view of politics?
tom	I object
judge	Objection overruled
prosecution	Your view of politics
tom	The sword of righteousness, the plough of good intent, the letterbox of hopefulness, the car of liberty, the mule of tourism, the mound of venus..
judge	I'm not convinced
tom	Love is impossible to explain, no-one understands
prosecution	(IN A SUDDEN FIT OF ANGER) What goddam use are you?
tom	The Lord said "make not strength a tool of your trade but weakness". Once I realised that I was well away. I became the mouthpiece of a nation. Not that that was any use to me
prosecution	No use you say and yet you did find some use for it did you not? In fact you were offered a mini-series
tom	That's not true your worship. I tried to dredge up something but nothing was there. I had a hand full of trumps but no card to lead with
prosecution	M'lud, he's not answering the question
judge	I must warn you that these weak arguments will gain you no favour with this court

tom	I enjoy the spite of selecting the weakest arguments to express my case. It's a way of emphasising its self-evidency
judge	(BITTERLY IRONIC) Very clever

THE JUDGE PLACES A BLACK CLOTH ON HIS HEAD

	Take him down!
court usher	The undersea kingdom awaits you sir, this way
tom	God knows I was espoused to fearlessness as a youth! In fact I was so impressed by what she showed me that I ran straight from her into the arms of pure terror...
gallery	Whatever happened to old Tom Doheny?
tom	...in whose luxuriant embrace I shall languish until my dying day...
judge	What a humiliating display, clear the court!
tom	Destiny, that last great master of disguise offered me a trick and I fell for it!
judge	What is the fellow talking about?
defence council	(CONFIDENTIALLY TO THE JUDGE) God's fool, the numbskull's right of intercession m'lud

RIOTOUS SCENES AS TOM DOHENY IS LED AWAY.

★   ★   ★

THE DRY MAN DRESSED UNCONVINCINGLY AS THE UNDERSEA EMPEROR LEADS TOM ALONG THROUGH THE WEEDS

dry man	Welcome to the undersea kingdom
tom	You don't fool me, this is a field of turnips
dry man	Nonsense. Didn't you see all those people we passed on our way waving their arms -
tom	- Fists
dry man	And that squireen that gave us a ride in his curricle
tom	You mean the squatter that threw us on the back with the pigs
dry man	We'll get there. You'll see the sky clouded with seaweed
tom	Oh to get out of here. I'd even beg forgiveness from my friends and family. Even the resentment of strangers would be a comfort -

dry man You see, above us only snow, below us African ground; this is the land of epitomes. Here it is no use to argue only to assuage. To be on the safe side call everything by its antonym, then everyone will understand

tom Is this where the Magic Bird comes into its own then?

dry man Not yet laddie, not yet. Learn to stand up on your own two feet, withered stumps though they be

tom You're joking I can tell. I've been dreaming. I shall wake up and it will be there again, I'll be home ...

HOME

TOM IS IN THE BATHROOM WRESTLING NELLIE'S HEAD UNDER THE BATH TAP. SHE IS IN HER MAGICIAN GEAR, HIGH HEELS, BLACK TIGHTS, WAISTCOAT, HER TOP HAT KNOCKED OFF AND ROLLING ON THE FLOOR. HE SCREAMS AT HER

tom For God's sake let me get the blood off your face!

nellie No! No!

(SUDDENLY HE SEES A SPIDER IN THE BATH AND SCREAMS IN TERROR)

tom Urgh! a spider!

(HE HIDES BEHIND HIS WIFE)

nellie Where?

tom Kill it! Kill it! Get rid of it!

(SUDDENLY, A MAN IN AN ANORAK WITH MANY ARMS GRABS HIM AROUND THE NECK AND BITES HIM)

tom Argh! Who the hell are you?

spider I'm the bloody spider

tom I always said they could bite, no-one believed me. (THE VICIOUS MAN-SPIDER HAS TOM'S HEAD IN A LOCK AND TWISTS IT WHILE HE RAVES)

spider You think you've got problems, my wife wants to eat me! You haven't known pain until you've begged for mercy and she's said 'I'll try'. It's not enough to cry your heart out, you must cut it out. But whatever you do with it thereafter it will always recognise birdsong, possibly as something malevolent but nevertheless familiar. (TWISTS HARDER)

tom	Argh!
spider	I open my mouth to utter the word 'freedom' and instead I say "close the door, close the door! hide me!" My head resounds with the clang of iron doors slamming. Each syllable has a thousand echoes
tom	For God's sake, let go of me!
spider	I look down in alarm at my hands to see they are clutching a spade digging my own grave, I turn to call for help but I find there only me, showing myself forward with a bitter sneer
tom	I can't help you, please, I'm an arachnophobe
spider	A dog runs at my heels and tries to bark but the poor brute can only whimper. I take pity on the dog and lower one of my hands to it but it tears at my fingers. (BITES HIS HAND)
tom	Argh!
spider	My wife doesn't know what romance is, but she's begging to know
tom	(CHOKING) Is she?
spider	I just hope she finds out in time

(NELLIE NOW SMACKS THE SPIDER IN THE BATH WITH HER SHOE SHE'D TAKEN OFF AND THE MAN-SPIDER SIMULTANEOUSLY FALLS BACKWARDS, DEAD)

nellie	Got it

IN THE TURNIP FIELD ONCE AGAIN

tom	Oh! (HE SHIVERS AND TREMBLES WITH DISGUST)
dry man	Don't you worry lad, I'll show you something new each day and when you're an old man you'll back on your life of experience and adventure and you'll say "I've lived"
tom	But who shall I say it to?
dry man	Some distant guardian of a distant gate. There'll always be someone there to light your way, have faith
tom	(IN TERROR) No, no! please help me, what can I do?

dry man   Alright, I'll tell you. this is it; Go and see a doctor, say to him, "doctor I've -

TOM IS IN A DOCTOR'S SURGERY

tom   - lost my nerve

doctor   So have I. Lost it long ago. That's why I'm sitting here. I gave up everything to be where you see me now. As you get older you make it impossible for yourself to see or hear anything new. The day is filled with things familiar to you until at last you feel you know your way about in this life, at that point you should realise you have surrendered to decay. And as you struggle to achieve the symbolic goal you have set yourself to convince you of your gameness, you desperately struggle to keep the balloon aloft by jettisoning ballast. This ballast though is Life Itself, you leave it behind you, strewn across the landscape of your unlived past. And the more you throw out, the lower the balloon sinks. Close your eyes, stand on one leg

DOES SO

Solid as a rock

TURNIP FIELD

tom   Actually as a matter of fact, now you mention it, we go onwards and onwards but each day you get sicker

dry man   (FOAMING AT THE MOUTH) Poor auld Tom Doheny, he thought up the magic bird, a cure for all ills upon us currently and he professed it until he became a fool. "alas"

tom   ... he said ...

dry man   ... the Magic Bird is dead, my intentions are dust and I must follow behind. Remember me

tom   But you had so many important things to say, where are they all?

dry man   Lost in my desire to be your slave little man

tom   If my friends could see me now

dry man   (HIDING HIS IRONY) Yes, yes, it's a great victory for you

tom	I quite enjoy this world you brought me into
dry man	The womb awaits you. Take me back with you
tom	No, no, this is wonderful. I've never in my life experienced one moment of abandon. But now I'm going to drink this
dry man	(IN HORROR) You madman! You liar! You've drunk my undersea kingdom dry!
tom	Puny liquor it is too. And me almost a tee-totaller
	AT ONCE THEY ARE AT SEA
tom	In a trice we are riding a foamy wave on the green ocean under a blue sky
dry man	It has its downside you know
tom	Don't tell me life has any limitations for the departing spirit. Suddenly you're staring freedom in the face
dry man	Don't remind me, liberty's crumbling dental arrangements have been grinning at me since I was in shorts
tom	... look at the gulls in our wake
dry man	... hungry blighters
tom	... flapping those giant wings of theirs
dry man	... I wish they wouldn't, they're working up a wind
tom	... in fact, hold on, they're whipping up a storm
dry man	... those damn birds!
tom	Hold on, we're going home. Who's that calling out below?
	ON BOARD SHIP IN A HEAVY SEA. TOM DOHENY IS ALOFT
jack tar	It's not the sea that galls us Tommy with it's hearty tossing, it's you aloft in your underpants in the crows nest all "land ahoy" and hopefulness. Your indominability in the face of certain death reminds us of the orphanage. Come down from there, there's a little thing we'd like to whisper in your red old ear that might interest you
tom	Call out if you've something to say, I think I spy land
'swain	(SHOUTING ABOVE THE FOAM) Well, we don't want to embarrass you

	but there's an old pig down here says you're his father. In the circumstances we'd like you to come and answer the charge of bestiality
tom	God damn yous! My life has been a long one, I can't remember every detail
'swain	It's not the obscenity in the normal sense that troubles us Tommy but you see it's the thought of your seed being wasted on dumb animals, we all … we all feel a bit insulted, don't we lads, especially the girls amongst us
tom	Is that a fact?
jack tar	It is Tommy, it is. Come down and meet your son
a pig	(AN EAGER SNORTING AND GRUNTING FROM BELOW)
tom	I will not. Don't you all want to be saved from this terrible storm?
an old salt	No it's alright, we're all insured
tom	(INSULTED) Oh. Didn't you trust your captain?
jack tar	How could we, with that old crow wrapped around you shoulders?
tom	This is the Magic Bird
old salt	It's dead
tom	Dead but clinging on nevertheless
old salt	Get that ill omened carcass out of there or we'll make you walk the plank
tom	You mutinous scoundrels! I'm the boss around here. You're forgetting perhaps who made this leaking hulk what it is today. You were nothing more than a glorified pleasure skiff full of ditch water until I took command. Now it will take the very eye of this typhoon to wreck us
undersea emperor	Ah let the poor deluded navvy sit up there if he wants to. What difference is it to us anyway, we're doomed men
tom	Watch out below, there's some big seas coming! There's one wave … and there's another
all abs as one	Oh merciful god!

tom   Let's see where your blackmailing pigs will get you now (HE LAUGHS
               BOLDLY AS THE SEAS OVERWHELM HIS SHIP)

jack tar   You wicked paddy! Why are you taking us to our destruction?
               We've been your hearties all this long trip, why pick on us?

tom   Ah it's a different tune now you're singing. Ha ha! (THE SEA ROLLS)
               We'll all go together! Hang on to your bulwarks!

               THE WILD SEAS RAGE, TOM DOHENY LAUGHS ALOFT

undersea emperor I'll get him down, I'll get him (SCALES THE MIZZEN) You wild
               man, I'll pull you down by God!

tom   Ah who's that down there, ha! the undersea emperor no less! So
               you'd scale my mizzen mast would you? Take that! (HE SWIPES AT HIM
               WITH THE CARCASS OF THE MAGIC BIRD)

magic bird   THE CARCASS SQUAWKS VAINLY

undersea emperor Your squawking carcass doesn't scare me boy!

               THE UNDERSEA EMPEROR ACHIEVES THE SUMMIT, THEY FIGHT

               Now my blue bearded rascal, got you! (HE HAS HIM ROUND THE NECK)
               Why don't you allow yourself the luxury of admitting you have
               always been hopelessly and undeniably a liar and a cheat, a blind
               beggar on the road to hell!

tom   I cannot accept your last generous offer. You alone are to blame for
               the wicked perversion of my miserable life

undersea emperor I'll dislodge you from your perch, you and your monstrous
               parrot

tom   If I go you'll go with me! and we'll drown together in the white-
               crested darkness of the sea

undersea emperor Let it be so!

               THEY TOPPLE AWAY, LOCKED IN MORTAL COMBAT

                              ★   ★   ★

               WASHED ASHORE, DISCOVERED ON THE BEACH BY HIS OLD FRIEND, THE PRIEST

tom   You think I'm sunbathing but in fact I'm shipwrecked and washed
               up upon the shore

priest	MUMBLES SOMETHING IN REPLY
tom	Where are my friends? They're strewn about here somewhere. At least they all came with me even if few survived the trip. They were all sea-faring men, God bless them. A refreshing change I can tell you after a life of landlubbers and Judases
priest	Don't you want to know where you are?
tom	It's all the same to me, my life is near its end, I have but a few words left to utter, a few scenes left to play. My repetoire is down to several wan smiles and a little wave (HE WAVES FEEBLY) like this
priest	Why man, you're drunk
tom	Yes! Ha! Yes indeed, my senses were stolen by the chateaux fonds of the lower vineyards. But excuse me do you know my wife? She'll want to know, she always wants to know, her love is such she will want to know
	(HE LOOKS OUT TO THE SURF)
	The sea, the sea, the roving sea, charms my destiny. Loneliness hangs upon me like an anchor chained on a cliff face
distant voice	Whatever happened to old Tom Doheny!
priest	You're in a fine state aren't you?
tom	My dear fella, you're a priest but there's no romance in your soul. I may have grown a beard and put on unfamiliar clothes but I am the same man underneath
priest	?
tom	I may have changed my mind and changed my heart but I am the same man underneath
priest	If not a heart or a mind what is a man? No more than a stomach?
tom	Then I am the same stomach
priest	Tell me do your old friends recognise you?
tom	Recognise me? They never knew me in the first place
priest	A man who cannot trust his friends is a man with a mean nature
tom	Or mean friends

priest	And your family, have they welcomed you back?
tom	Surely. They sent money for my ticket and begged me to come home. Now of course they ignore me. You can't expect miracles. Anyway at least it was a touching scene as the bigot rescued me from my persecutors
priest	What? You faced a mutiny?
tom	The boat I was on sunk many times. Waves as big as houses engulfed us time after time. Prayer was futile, there was nothing for it but to man the pumps
priest	Ah I am no stranger to the bilges myself. The ship's biscuit and the holy sacrament have been the twin cakes of my sustenance on this earth
tom	Who ever heard of a priest on the yard arm. A clergyman at sea is useless. Rather than binding his wrists to the wheel he would rather strap himself to the mast in imitation of his master. I must leave you now and write a letter. The hour prior to sleep is my best writing hour. I strap myself to the mast of my pen while the waves of my unconscious rise up about me. I awake in the morning to see the inky measure of their wrath on the page beside me
priest	Is it any wonder she despises you. She wants a highway in the sand, you give her shipwrecks from your pillow

★   ★   ★

AN OLD BIDDY TALKING TO HERSELF. A FAMILAR BICYCLE IS LEANING AGAINST THE WALL. SHE IS TENDING GERANIUMS IN POTS

biddy	..and then there's loads of dem dere don't want to work, mind over matter or whatever you may call it..

A PASSIONATE PLEA COMES FROM OLD TOM IN A WHEELBARROW WHEELED BY THE PRIEST

tom	Tell her, tell her for God's sake. She may laugh at these stained vest and pants now but in our youth she was glad enough of them, couldn't keep her chapped fingers out of them as I recall. Those red rings round her eyes were once moist fairy rings of delight. For God's sake woman what good is there in leaving it like this?

biddy	Oh John-Joe how I loved thee!
tom	Get off, get off, I'm not him! You liar, you old braggart! We won't trouble your ladyship just let us rest here awhile in your roses
biddy	Rest there all you like, you can bury yourselves underneath 'em for all I care. They need a good peating
tom	Oh so you see me as a source of manure now. There was a time.. So if here amongst your roses I remain, anyway you'll not be long for this world..
biddy	(TO PRIEST) Tell me sir, is it a meal you're begging? For I've some old stew in a can I could bring out, save him bothering the neighbours with his chanting
tom	Stew is a magnificent thing to be sure, but we were hoping for something a little more vital
biddy	Not forgiveness I hope
tom	No, not that. Not that but recognition
biddy	Recognition you may have and take away with you all you may find and never come back with it, so I can live peacefully and forget all about out it
tom	She doesn't understand a word we're saying. Surely you have some recollection woman of the love we shared together
biddy	Huh, how could I forget, wasn't it that put me here to rot forever on my own?
tom	Precisely, precisely, which is why madam I have come to join you now, Christ she's slow on the uptake
priest	Tom, this isn't getting us anywhere, let's move on
tom	God damn you! I may have misled you, deserted you, abandoned you, robbed you of happiness, left you to lead a life of lonely sorrow and deprived you of any children we might have had, but you couldn't say I haven't loved you!
biddy	Call that love!
tom	And what do you call this? The scar on my thigh where you plunged your knife
biddy	(PEERS) All I see is a mass of grey hairs (SHE WEEPS, STROKES HIS LEG) Oh

Tom, Tom what a fine leg you always had! I never could look at your shabby body without wanting you!

(THEY EMBRACE WITH TEARS)

tom	Ah Bridget, Bridget, my own sweet girl what has happened your hair? She was as gold as the dawn from head to foot. And you're as fat as the bog itself
biddy	I told you I'd grow round like a ball, I like it
tom	Oh so do I, so do I!
biddy	Come on round the back with me now and I'll lift my skirts for you like I used

SHE DISAPPEARS

tom	I must go with her
priest	(HELPS HIM TO HESITATE) You can't go in your vest. Hadn't you better borrow my big coat?
tom	What would I be wanting a coat for?
priest	To take off. You must have something to take off for the full effect, to sweep her up in, they like to be swept up and those thin arms of yours won't be doing much sweeping will they?
tom	After all these years. Not a night has gone by that I haven't longed for her. My throat has gone all sticky with the thought of her
priest	Why dally then, off you go
tom	..Because she always cries so sorrowfully everytime, it breaks my heart to see her. And then she drifts away, looking over my shoulder and I'm left alone like a fool
priest	You're afraid of the great well of emotion inside her
tom	Nonsense, I'm not afraid of that, I can match her. God we used to roll around when we were young, you wouldn't credit it. And laugh! by Christ. And I'll tell you one thing, I have paid in suffering for every moment spent with her, I've no debt to pay on that score
priest	Go on then she's waiting
tom	I'll bet she's as hot now as she was then

priest	I'll bet
tom	It was something came entirely natural to her like breathing
priest	She was certainly the girl for you sounds like
tom	For me? Oh God she was never mine. Never, never mine. Or was she? In a sense she was. And still is. There is a secret bond to be sure, in a dimension invisible to the men and women of this earth
priest	A bond of immense joy
tom	And immense sorrow
priest	If you take her now maybe she'll be yours forever
tom	Oh no, you don't know her, she's a fierce girl, oh yes don't worry about that, she'll not be giving herself for nothing no more, she's tried that and was bitterly burnt. I could no more have her for my own than I could the hills over there or the rivers that run between
priest	Independent is she?
tom	What? Go and ask her and she'll give you a thick ear for your trouble. No men will ever come near her, no man in my opinion is good enough to even sit and drink her watery tea (her tea which I grant is filth). She has the dignity of a tigress and the sweetness of a cub, the shoulders of a venus, the mouth of a fish, the breath of a whore, the eye of a poem, the foot of a cripple, the breast of a dove, the nose of a navvy, the heart of an oyster, and I am a herring, do you hear me a herring, floating headless on its back, this way and that on the ocean's tides....
priest	I can see you're too in love to function. Would you like me to go and tell her?
tom	Never, never! I've not failed her yet and I won't now. Just give me a help out of this wheelbarrow
	DOES SO
biddy	(REAPPEARING) It's no good Tommy, I can't go through with it, it will leave me red and raw like it always did and I don't want to feel the pain of loss today of all days no thankyou for I have other troubles

49

tom	You've always had your troubles my love and it kills me that I cannot help you
biddy	It kills me too but there it is. You'll have to go now, my child is sick and I must away to her with some herbs
tom	Is there any way I can help you, any way at all? I hate to see you labouring, you look tired and drawn
biddy	That's nothing but age. Off with you now. Come back soon and see me and don't look so sorrowful

THEY STAGGER AWAY

tom	Enough of despondancy - Now of exhillaration, come I'll show you a fine thing

HE STOPS

I now realise that you will find my pleasures are only weaknesses indulged to the point of enjoyment but, I ask you... oh well here she comes...

NELLIE APPEARS DRESSED IN A TOP HAT AND HIGH HEELS. COMES AND PERFORMS A SULLEN MAGIC TRICK WITH EXTREME GRACE. HER CANE TURNS TO A HANDKERCHIEF THEN TO A DOVE, FLUTTERING WINGS ACCOMPANIED BY A CLANKING PIANO

priest	Why that's amazing!
tom	This is Nellie, you remember her
priest	Of course
tom	She has promised to teach me tricks too. Haven't you

SHE SMILES BUT NOT IN RESPONSE TO HIS QUESTION

priest	She's very beautiful
tom	Make us all disappear

DOES SO

First performed at Leicester Haymarket Studio in June 1989

Looking At You (revived) Again

ABE COMES INTO VIEW. HE IS FORTY YEARS OLD AND WEARS AN OLD DOUBLE
BREASTED SUIT WITH A YELLOW FLOWER IN THE LAPEL. HIS DIRTY DARK HAIR
IS TUCKED BEHIND HIS EARS AND REACHES HIS COLLAR. HE HAS A SLIGHT LIMP

HE AMBLES ALONG, IS ABOUT TO SPEAK WHEN PERAGRIN'S DAUGHTER
ARRIVES AT HIS ELBOW. SHE IS YOUNG AND DIRTY AND TIRED OUT

ABE GOES AND STANDS NEXT TO THE DARK WOMAN. SHE HAS FLAMING RED
HAIR WITH DARK BROWN ROOTS AND WEARS PALE SHADED GLASSES. HER OLD
NYLON TRACK SUIT TOP IS GREASY AND SO ARE HER TROUSERS. FOR THE
MOMENT SHE WEARS A BRIDAL VEIL ATOP HER HAIR

abe   This land is full of fine women. Full of fine people

The love of a good woman. Keep the wolf from your door

'Step up O'driscoll to the altar

Where'll we find a priest? Ask in the vestry.

At this time of the morning? He's fast asleep in his hammock.

What time is it? Six o'clock. Six o'clock in the morning.

Well tell him Dermot, the charmer of all England is here

wanting to take the pledge and get married.

They won't let you. They won't let you

not with the smell of John Barleycorn on your teeth.'

'Alright then, I'll take my teeth out.'

Got a big laugh, that one

'Come on lads, jostle him up the aisle. What a roaring party
we've got here!

And who's that standing by the altar rail in a sunbeam?

In the slanted rays of the dawn sun?

Why, it's Mrs James.'

The love of a very good woman

'We've had some laughs with Mrs James haven't we lads?

Why does she call herself that? Wanted to impress.

She's in love with him. In love!'

Mrs James stood in a sunbeam, her flaming red hair, roots like ashes.

I knew it was not to be.

'Quick lads, quick, stand them together. Light those candles!

At half past six they dragged the priest away from his sleeping pillow and pulled and antimacassock over his head and brought him screaming blue murder to the alter, his neck in a halter.

My bride. Oh my bride

★   ★   ★

P.D JOINS ABE WITH A GUITAR

abe	OK
p.d	Yeah, yeah. Hmmm
abe	OK (PUTS HIS HAND OUT FOR THE GUITAR)
p.d	Eh? Oh yeah (HANDS HIM A BOTTLE)
abe	No
p.d	Oh. Oh yeah (HANDS HIM THE GUITAR)
abe	Unpack it then
p.d	Ah! (SIGHS) Yeah. Yeah (NERVOUSLY UNPACKS THE GUITAR FROM ITS CASE)
abe	Right (PAUSE. HE LOOKS AT HER)
p.d	Oh (MOVES BACK AWAY BEHIND A POST)
abe	What have you been doing to it?
p.d	Oh
abe	What?

p.d	It's out of tune isn't it
abe	Yeah its out of tune
p.d	Whew! Hey, do you want some?
abe	What's the matter?
p.d	Hot. It's hot
abe	This is out of tune, you must have bumped it
p.d	Ah. (SIGHS) Yeah, I bumped it I think. Whew! (DRINKS)
abe	Ah. (SIGHS) Where's the bag?
p.d	Here, here! (HOLDS IT OUT)
abe	Yep. The bag has got to be here, with me for the coins to fall into
p.d	Abe
abe	Yes my dear?
p.d	Play a song
abe	I'm going to. I need a new string
p.d	Mm (BITES HER LIP, STRAIGHTENS HER SLEEVE, SITS DOWN)
abe	People
p.d	Where? (GETTING UP)
abe	It looks bad, you've got to stand up. And away (WAVES HER AWAY)
p.d	(WORRIED) Oh Abe!
abe	You'll be alright
p.d	OK (STRAIGHTENS HER SLEEVE, PUTS HER HAIR BEHIND HER EAR)
abe	(FINDS A NEW STRING, TUNES UP)
p.d	Abe, Abe
abe	Mm?
p.d	Can we go?
abe	We only just arrived
p.d	I know. I know we did. But. Yeah
	PAUSE
	Abe, can we go now?
abe	Ow! I broke my finger nail

p.d   Abe

★   ★   ★

ABE JOINS THE DARK WOMAN

abe   Outside the crowds of creditors gathered calling my name and blowing their whistles in the cold morning air. And inside the church, squatting behind statues, their agents, bailiffs, mad dogs of women, anyone with a grievance against me, all hiding there unnoticed in the merry throng

Does a poor man deserve to marry in the clear sunlight of a spring morning?

In a little city church with black walls and bedecked with flowers? They hired a piper to play, we even borrowed a ring for the poor girls finger.

We shoved the man of God into his church and pressed the word of God into his hand.

'Don't be paying any mind to that lot outside. It's just the local residents complaining about the hullabaloo. The traffic has come to a halt outside y'know, oh yes. There are hordes of them out there. How do you know so many people? They want your blood. We've just had word from the police that they can't guarantee our protection. Better crank that priest up a bit.

Come on your holyship, spit the words out!'

Thump, thump, thump! Bang, bang, bang!

ABE CLUTCHES ONTO THE DARK WOMAN'S ARM IN FRIGHT. SHE STARES AHEAD HOPEFULLY

Someone's a-thumping on the doors. Don't let them in Mary!

'Driscoll,' thundered the voice from outside. 'What about your little farm you left behind at home? The pigs lay dying, go home and feed them!'

Yes, and do you know why??! You businessmen have bought up my little farm and turned it into a slaughter-house. You developed me! And now I'm in debt

'Don't lie Driscoll, for we all know that you left your little farm and the little piggies without a word of goodbye, and went off to seek your fortune. We all know that Driscoll, ask your poor mam!'

Mammy, mammy

'Oh yes Driscoll. You went off to some fine place didn't you!'
Yes! And what did I find when I got there?
You! You lot were there waiting for me, dogging my every step. You owned the very ground I walked on.

Don't heed them my love. We'll be married don't you fret

dark woman I hear you don't have any collateral. I suppose you haven't even the price of a bowl of soup

abe A bowl of soup my love? Are you hungry? If you can just hold on the bridal breakfast will be ready for you.

'Look out Mrs James is putting him through his paces. Look at him jump! Oh well, isn't she a fine one, when you consider that the trousers she's got on her are dripping grease'

'Never you mind all that now Driscoll. The thing is you owe us some rent..'

Go to the devil for your rent!

HE SHAKES HIS FIST ABOUT HIM IN ALL DIRECTIONS

Bang! Bang! Thump!

More banging?

'Do you think they'll bust the doors down? Do you think they will? Scandalous!'

'Driscoll. Driscoll?'

What is it?

'And where will you be living with your bride?'

Never mind that! Never mind that! Leave me alone! We have a place don't you worry!

'Oh yes? And would that be a little house with a blue door and a few broken windows where we've seen you of late?'

I don't know what colour the door is!

'But Driscoll! You shouldn't be in that house! No, no, because it's

57

not your own! You don't seriously think you can squat your little arse down on those floorboards do you?'

Why ever not? (WEAKLY)

'You must know surely that we own that house Driscoll'

★   ★   ★

PERAGRIN'S DAUGHTER AT HIS ELBOW ON THE LEFT HAND SIDE

p.d	I need a toilet
abe	You've already been this morning
p.d	(SHAKES HER HEAD AND WHIMPERS A BIT)
abe	Go in the station
p.d	Yeah. You come with me
abe	No go on, you go, you'll be alright
p.d	You go with me
abe	What's the matter? Are you feeling nervous?
p.d	(STARES AHEAD, THINKS, MOVES HER HAIR, STRAIGHTENS HER SLEEVE) Yeah, yeah (NODS)
abe	Alright. Just go to the toilet. I'll wait here and then we'll start, OK? Everything will be fine
p.d	No, it's alright. I'll wait
abe	OK

★   ★   ★

abe	(SEIZES P.D) And with that the little devils rose up from behind the statues of the Mother of God in the middle of our ceremony and four and twenty mad women danced towards me and seized me by the arms and dragged me through the bewildered crowd of my wedding guests, and raised me up onto their shoulders like I was a coffin and did a jig out through the doors bearing me aloft and delivered me up to my enemies. It was all over
p.d	Mind your guitar
abe	But saddest of all, the last sight I saw, was out of the corner of my eye as they carried me away; my weeping bride, her red, red hair

falling down into her face, fainting into the arms of the black suited bailiffs, the borrowed ring slipping from her finger

THE DARK WOMAN DRIFTS AWAY

p.d   What's the matter?

abe   I think I can see the back door. The future that used to be ahead is already in the past without ever having been in the present

p.d   Would you like a drink from my bottle?

SHE FEEDS HIM IT

There, drink it back. That's it

abe   How like my mother you sound. And you so young. Don't start mothering until your teats are properly developed or you'll have trouble later on

p.d   Come home with me

abe   You haven't a home

p.d   I'd like to have one

abe   That's where we are different. I have one but I can't go to it.

I've been on the road now many a year, hounded from lay-by to lay-by

I'd love to give up the roaming life. Perhaps go back and find the woman who...

I left her to fend for herself. I've heard she's wandering about in this vicinity herself these days.

I hope one day to run into her

I met an old boy the other day said she's quite well to-do now. I don't know how he would know. Still, I trust she's been faithful. She hadn't much option with the eight kids I left on her lap

p.d   (SHE TUCKS HER HAIR BEHIND HER EAR AND STRAIGHTENS HER SLEEVE)

abe   Yes, it's a fine thing. Of course ours are scattered to the four corners of the earth; residing in orphanages under false names

How will we ever get them back? It's all I live for but they're hidden from us. They are brainwashing them I expect, turning them against us. It's the old story. I expect to be arrested by one of my sons one day

'Son,' I'll say, 'go on put the shackles on me.' And he'll say, 'Daddy, why did you leave us alone in the trailer undernourished and starving like you did?'

What good telling him I was walking up the road to fetch water and a few bottles of milk when the social worker stole them away. How could the little ones understand that?

'You didn't love us, Daddy,' he'll say. 'If you had loved us you wouldn't have let them take us away.'

What good saying I was tricked by the constables and held by the arms in the police station?

p.d	You can have new children with me
abe	New children? I'm afraid... no, you're too young. For all I know you could be my own
p.d	Grandchildren then, have grandchildren with me
abe	(SUDDENLY LOST) Where are we? Where are we going?
p.d	You're with me. I'll look after you
abe	You? Who are you? Can you spare a pound?
p.d	Yes, yes, look (SHE STRUGGLES A FEW COINS FROM HER POCKET)
abe	(HE STARES AT HER DIRTY PALM) God bless you, it's not enough. Keep it. Save it up. Add to it. Then one day you'll have a pound
p.d	I'll help you find her
abe	No, no, I know where she is
p.d	I've already had many children. Growing. In here. Do you see my hair?
abe	Your hair, yes...
p.d	It's different today -
abe	Child -
p.d	It could be. Look. (SHE SPLAYS OUT HER LANK HAIR IN HER FINGERS) It is isn't it? It means there's another one growing inside
abe	Let me go

p.d   Are you going now?

abe   Am I going now? Yes, yes. I'm going. Just help me rest a while first, then I'll go. Move those things so I can sit down

p.d   There isn't anything

abe   Isn't there? I thought there was something

p.d   (PREPARES FOR HIM TO SIT DOWN. HE DOESN'T. SHE TUCKS HER HAIR BEHIND HER EAR, SHE STRAIGHTENS HER SLEEVE) I feel like a lioness

abe   When you are both very tired, an extra companion can join you, or sometimes just a piece of luggage. It's an hallucination

★   ★   ★

THE DARK WOMAN WHEELS UP AND DOWN ON HER BALCONY. ABE IS IN THE STREET BELOW

abe   'Open this door! (HE THUMPS THE DOOR, HE LAUGHS) Open up!'

dark woman   (SHE LIFTS HERSELF OUT OF HER WHEELCHAIR AND HANGS OVER THE BALCONY THEN SLUMPS BACK INTO HER CHAIR) Oh it's you

abe   'It's the bailiffs, come to get you out'

dark woman   'Oh yes, well, I'm occupied in drawing up my husband's accounts Your Lordship'

abe   'I shall be wanting to look at those infamous documents too!'

dark woman   'They're nearly finished but not quite'

abe   'Then madam I must conclude that you can barely be numerate'

dark woman   Don't start flaunting your airs and graces!

abe   'Come on out of there you old biddy!'

dark woman   Don't push your luck (SHE THROWS A BOTTLE AT HIM) Clear off!

abe   You don't want to end up an old soak on the streets but then, who does? And then, why shouldn't it be you? I don't see you inviting the homeless in off the streets

dark woman   (TRYING TO LIFT HERSELF UP IN AGITATION) Liar! Just give me the power to walk and you'll never see me again. You can keep the rotten stinking house, I don't want it!

abe   But you can walk surely?

dark woman	(IN TEARS, ANGRY) I can't, I can't!
abe	Oh come on now, a little bit surely ...
dark woman	I can't Why don't you look at this - (SHE CRIES, THUMPING HER WHEELCHAIR)
	PAUSE
abe	'Ah, now we're not hard men. Tell us, you must have had a little accident, no?'
dark woman	'I did Sir, yes. An accident with the stairs. Long ago. And I'm still a cripple from it'
abe	'Oh is that so? Yes, that's bad'
dark woman	(CRIES) Yes, I can't bloody walk!
abe	'It's a pity because we want the house. It's your husband you see. Never paid a debt since the day you married him. Could you tell me why that is?'
dark woman	'Well the truth of it is Your Lordship, he has no money'
abe	'Ah, no money, no money, poor man. Well, if you could see your way to helping us out with a few bob on his behalf it will go favourably for him when we next consider his case'
dark woman	Consider his case all you want, it's nothing to do with me
abe	But a few pence to keep body and soul together ...
dark woman	I have nothing!
abe	Alright then, I'll leave you here in your shame!
dark woman	There's no shame here except the shame of he who left me
abe	I wish I could believe that
dark woman	STARTS COUGHING
abe	What's the matter?
dark woman	Nothing (COUGHS MORE)
abe	You should rest. Stay inside in the warm
dark woman	Shut up. I don't want to
	SHE COUGHS HERSELF INTO EXHAUSTION

★　　★　　★

ABE TURNS TO P.D WHO TURNS AWAY

abe   Well my child, what can I do for you?

You do recognize me I hope?

I am a married man as you can see

Hand me my stick can you boy. Thankee

I have suffered a few little bits of damage to my leg on account of things not being properly screwed down on deck

Whoops! (HE REELS AND REGAINS HIS BALANCE AS IF THEY ARE ON A SHIP)

What have we here? A cabin boy? Your hair is exceeding long. Come with me boy ...

P.D TUCKS HER HAIR BEHIND HER EAR AND STRAIGHTENS HER SLEEVE

abe   Don't worry (HE TAKES A FEW STEPS AWAY AND ROLLS A CIGARETTE)

THEY STAND STARING IN OPPOSITE DIRECTIONS UNABLE TO TALK. P.D STEALS A GLANCE AT HIS BACK THEN HE TURNS AND LOOKS OVER HIS SHOULDER

abe   Hello there

p.d   LOOKS AWAY

ABE TURNS TO HER HOLDING HIS CIGARETTE

abe   If you ask me I'd say you don't look very well

p.d   LOOKS AT HIM STRAIGHTENS HER SLEEVE, TUCKS HER HAIR BEHIND HER EAR AND TURNS AWAY

abe   Got a light?

p.d   SEARCHES HER POCKETS

abe   (GOES TO HER) The ship I was on, the Captain had smuggled his wife on board dressed as a cabin boy. This was bringing the ship bad luck, and in the middle of a great tempest we forced him to confess his deception. We made him tie her up and throw her overboard, to save all our lives. Poor man how he wept lamenting his selfishness. (HE TAKES P.D BY THE SHOULDERS AND INDICATES THE SEA WITH HIS ARM) And in the very moment that the girl's white dresses were bobbing around in the waves the waters became calm again

p.d   STRAIGHTENS HER SLEEVE

abe   Yes, calm waters

p.d   STRIKES HIM A MATCH

abe   Thankee

Aren't you a little big young to be out on the streets on your own?

A DOG BARKS IN A BACK YARD FAR AWAY

The debt she has is all my own

THE DOG BARKS SOME MORE

But as you can see, she has reached levels of hypocrisy and chicanery that leaves the likes of me, a simple working man, a peasant by birth, leaves me standing

p.d   Let's go, Abe

abe   It's a wild life isn't it? People here, people there. Who can tell? Who knows what's going on eh? Who knows?

I've been around

p.d   Abe -

abe   (TO HIMSELF ABOUT P.D) Funny thing is, when you get up close she's got a peculiar smell

p.d   ?

abe   Like a fox's arse. An attractive person all in all, but aromatic, in an odd way

We shall play truant together. You play truant, I'll collect the social security

Thank goodness I'm here to help you

p.d   Yes

abe   Where's your daddy?

p.d   Daddy ...

abe   He should be here to protect you, shouldn't he? Should I take you to the sea? Can you drive? No? A pity, we could have gone on holiday together

p.d	I don't want to go on holiday with you -
abe	Why not?
p.d	(IN A SUDDEN OUTBURST) You keep writing all your letters to me telling me what great friends we are but you could be mistaken - That's why!
abe	(TAKEN ABACK) But I've never written a letter to you in my life. Why, I hardly know you
p.d	(HOLDING HER HANDS IN FRONT OF HER FACE) Sorry! The letters you leave for her
abe	You've been reading my letters?
p.d	You never seal them
abe	No, I never seal them. It thrills me to think that others might read them
p.d	They're beautiful letters ...
abe	I'm just glad somebody reads them. They are composed by the engine-room mechanic. He's a romantic genius. Talking of genius. Have I shown you this?

HE PRODUCES A NEWSPAPER CUTTING FROM HIS POCKET AND HANDS IT TO HER

	It's a friend of mine actually. Seems to be doing rather well doesn't he. We were at school together. Great pals
p.d	(CHECKING BOTH SIDES) It's an advertisement
abe	What? Here. Let me see (HE SNATCHES IT) I've cut out the wrong bit!

★   ★   ★

NIGHT-TIME. ABE LEADS P.D

abe	Look, it's early evening. There's no moon. It's very dark. That's just how I like it.
	You see this line of trees?
p.d	No
abe	Let's just say there's a line of trees. Strange trees, short, knotted, like dwarfed trees

p.d	Yes
abe	I must say, it rather spoils the effect that you can't see them. Surely your young eyes...?
p.d	(LOOKS VAGUELY)
abe	Alright
p.d	Listen, can you help me?
abe	Well
p.d	I need a drink
abe	It's easy. Just hold your breath, tip your head back...
p.d	(FAINTS, HE CATCHES HER)
abe	You shouldn't roll your eyes too far back into your head
	SHE COMES TO
	Look on the bright side, this can't go on forever
p.d	Take me home
abe	I can't. Whoops! (HE REELS AGAIN THEN BALANCES AS IF THEY ARE ON A SHIP) Look at that. We've hit a storm
p.d	(PRODUCES A BOTTLE) Rum?
abe	Certainly
p.d	I have to go to the toilet
abe	You go too often, it makes you thin. Try to slow down your metabolism
p.d	My doctor says I have a fast heartbeat. Feel
abe	I'm not a doctor. I wouldn't know where to look
p.d	Here (SHE PUTS HIS HAND TO THE JUGULAR VEIN IN HER NECK)
abe	(IMMEDIATELY) Very fast. Perhaps you should sit down
p.d	And here (UNDER HER BREAST)
abe	... my life is... I'd like to explain
p.d	I'd like to go to the toilet
abe	I went to her father. Father-in-law, I said, lend me a thousand pounds. I can't, he said, I have responsibilities to my race, we

are a wandering tribe. I gave him ten pounds of my own and said, 'Take this and wander away as far as you like.' She's from a persecuted people

A LORRY GOES PAST, IT HAS A WHINING WHEEL THAT SCREAMS LOUDLY, FADES

p.d	(TAKES A FEW STEPS) I like cities
abe	So do I
p.d	They make me feel so warm inside
abe	Where are you going?
p.d	So warm inside
abe	And of course that business with the pigs. Men in suits kept coming around and bothering her when I wasn't there to protect her. They tried to shift all the blame for that onto her shoulders. They sent her photographs, horrible, horrible things, with demands for payment. I don't deny it made her life a misery
p.d	I'm feeling the inside of my cage
abe	And what with the children running about all over the place from God knows where, booted around from corner to corner
p.d	I'm like a wounded animal in the zoo
abe	I must go
p.d	Let me come with you
abe	With me? I would but I'm not really going anywhere.

PAUSE

	Let me give you a little advice
p.d	Not now
abe	Why not?
p.d	I'm haemorrhaging
abe	The advice is this ...
p.d	CRIES IN PAIN
abe	If you ever let something take root in you ...

p.d	Am I having a baby?
abe	... It'll be like one of those trees
p.d	Oh! (IN PAIN)
abe	Strange old pixies of trees aren't they?
p.d	Please ...
abe	Oh God!

HE HOLDS HER FAINTING IN HIS ARMS

abe	How long will this go on for?
p.d	This is your fault
abe	(HOLDS HER) My poor child. Don't worry. I was attracted by your negative qualities. You, you fill up the dark side of a man. You are the invisible side of my soul
p.d	Do you love me?
abe	Love?
p.d	All men love me
abe	You're mistaken ...
p.d	Abe
abe	Ester, Ester, help me
p.d	Who's that you're calling?
abe	My wife. She did first aid I remember

P.D COLLAPSES

abe	Get up, get up, I'm not finished. Gentle soul. She deserves better than this.
	I thought somehow I could encourage you with my positive qualities you see and that between us a more or less equal librium would be established until we got you to a toilet or even something better, who knows.
	But now. Oh get up please!
p.d	(MUTTERING) All men love me
abe	Hush, hush, who needs to know that?

★ ★ ★

68

ABE WHEELS THE DARK WOMAN IN HER WHEELCHAIR, THEY COME
THROUGH THE DOOR AND ALONG THE BALCONY. ABE WHEELS SLOWLY.
THE DARK WOMAN HAS SUNGLASSES ON. THE BRIGHT MORNING SUN
SHINES ONTO HER FACE. SHE SQUINTS INTO IT, BRUSHING THE HAIR BACK
OFF HER CHEEKS

abe   Coffee?

dark woman   Mm

abe   Doughnuts?

dark woman   Mm yes!

ABE GOES IN

A LORRY GOES BY WITH A WHINING WHEEL

SOUND OF CHILDREN PLAYING COME DRIFTING FROM A SCHOOL PLAY-
GROUND

THE DARK WOMAN LEANS ON THE BALCONY SUNNING HER FACE, LISTEN-
ING AND WATCHING

ABE REAPPEARS. TWO COFFEES, DOUGHNUTS IN A PAPER BAG

dark woman   Where did you get them?

abe   I nipped out earlier while you were still asleep

dark woman   Then you came back and scared me

abe   You thought I was the police

dark woman   Yes I did

abe   Doughnuts?

dark woman   Thanks

abe   Coffee

dark woman   Isn't it a wonderful morning

abe   Yes, yes it is

dark woman   It is, Abe

PAUSE

It's nice of you to wheel me around a bit this morning, my
fingers ache so much ... Abe?

abe	Yes?
dark woman	There is a thing you could do for me. I'd love it ...
abe	What?
dark woman	Lift me out of this chair
abe	Lift you?
dark woman	Pick me up. Take me in your arms as if I were your little daughter or something and hold me up so I can see over the balcony rail. Would you do that?
abe	I'll do that ...
dark woman	(STARES AT HIM AND SMILES) I'll just put down my coffee cup. There. Alright. I'm ready
abe	LIFTS HER OUT OF HER WHEELCHAIR
	THEY STARE AT EACH OTHER
abe	Aren't you going to look then?
dark woman	Look? Oh yes, yes (SHE DOESN'T LOOK) Put me down please Abe
abe	Down?
dark woman	Yes please
abe	(HE SETS HER DOWN IN THE WHEELCHAIR AGAIN. PAUSE) Well, what did you see?
dark woman	(HOLDING HER HEAD IN HER HANDS) Nothing
abe	You want to get out and about a bit
dark woman	You say that! I never wanted to live here. You brought me here against my will
abe	I did not
dark woman	Against my will!
abe	This was our home
dark woman	Not to me it wasn't
abe	Not to you
dark woman	Don't try to be surprised
abe	I'm not surprised

dark woman	You shouldn't be! Locking me in here!
abe	I'm sorry ... I wasn't able to be here with you ... more often
dark woman	You never lived here!
abe	No, sadly
dark woman	Oh yes, the great man, free to roam
abe	Exiled
dark woman	Oh your fine words! Your find words! And all your friends and all your women -
abe	I have no friends. And all the women I have kissed goodbye long ago
dark woman	While I rot!
abe	I promise you I am as lonely as you
dark woman	Rot in this ditch
abe	It was to be our marital ditch
dark woman	I never wanted it. You'd have me a little bird on your window sill
abe	A little bird?
dark woman	These are walls of a prison to me. This is not the way of my people. I want the whisper of the moon, the trickle of the old fawcet ...
abe	Well, you've been here so long now so why not stop complaining? If I could I'd help you. I'd do anything. But what can I do? You're in that chair and well, we're stuck with it
dark woman	(WITH VENOM) Don't mention the chair
abe	I should mention it
dark woman	Oh you love it don't you!
abe	It's our problem isn't it ...
dark woman	Oh yes!
abe	And because of it you can't ever leave the house. It's true, I have to say it
dark woman	Don't ... just don't

abe	Don't what woman?
dark woman	Don't ...
abe	You are bitter. You are. Bitter. I don't blame you. I'd be bitter
dark woman	... dare
abe	It's the drink talking now
dark woman	You - !
abe	Isn't it?
dark woman	Oh yes, the fine man! Tell me. Tell me more, what shall I do daddio. What would you advise that I do? Do you have any great ideas?
abe	It was you, drunk, fell down the stairs
dark woman	Oh yes!
abe	Down the stairs and broke your back
dark woman	Oh was it? Was it really?
abe	Oh God, can you see it now? The little children standing outside for the ambulance. Oh our Mammy has broken her neck and she's going to be dead. Oh our Mammy nearly killed our poor dad as well with a kitchen knife when he tired to stop her
dark woman	STARTS UP A SCREAM
abe	Oh our Mammy is screaming now as she screamed then. Isn't she? Doesn't she scream with the best of them? And didn't we once hear her say Daddy doesn't touch her no more. And is that a dirty thing? Because Daddy seemed ashamed
dark woman	(A HIGH PITCHED WAIL) Go away!
abe	Then you drove the little kiddies away. And now they'll never come back
dark woman	I did not not drive them away!
abe	As soon as my back was turned. I'd only just popped out. Cast them out!
dark woman	No, no Abe
abe	I was only just fetching a loaf of bread and some matches!

dark woman	Oh you're so cruel!
abe	The little darlings, we haven't seen them since. It backfired on you didn't it, your dirty trick? You couldn't get them back could you?
dark woman	It was the police took them, and that woman with glasses, they threw them in the van
abe	That was your revenge wasn't it?
dark woman	No, no they was screaming to me, 'Mam! Mam!' They knew I wanted them to stay. The police held me back, they pushed me on the floor.
abe	You fell over, you were too drunk
dark woman	It was in the morning, I hadn't had a drink. I was, I was looking for their breakfast
abe	There wasn't any breakfast
dark woman	I was looking ...
abe	There was nothing except margarine
dark woman	Yes and why was that? You'd not bought any food, not even for your own children could you produce even a bit of bread and milk
abe	How could I? There was no money
dark woman	No money! Why didn't you earn some money
abe	I tried!
dark woman	Oh yes, you tried. You couldn't even feed your own children
abe	They wouldn't let me on the gangs
dark woman	They could see what kind you were
abe	They wouldn't let me ...
dark woman	Good enough for you!
abe	You wicked woman!
dark woman	Oh yes I'm wicked. Didn't you know? I'm evil actually. Watch out I don't put a spell on you
abe	You've already done that. My whole life, my children

dark woman	I put a spell on my own children? I'll kill you if you don't get out
abe	Kill me, I don't care. It will be a relief to all of us
dark woman	And listen to the self pity now. Listen to the self pity of the man who couldn't keep his children from the law

PAUSE

★   ★   ★

A ROADSIDE. A LINE OF WASHING STRUNG FROM ONE TREE TO ANOTHER. RAIN IS FALLING

abe	It was very dull to live in a country where there is nothing. You're never ahead. Always behind

PAUSE

Poverty is a terrible thing.

That's what I like about this place. Everyone is so rich.

It's wonderful

PAUSE

I suppose my washing is wet from the rain

p.d	Yeah, it got wet
abe	Never mind. We'll have to get a lift in to a launderette. In town. We'll get a lift in a lorry (STANDS UP)
	I like the countryside. It makes you feel so warm. Inside
p.d	Where are we going?
abe	I'm just glad to get some fresh air. I belong to the wind, I'm at home in the mud and the fields, when the trees are dripping water, I'm at home. On the day I left, didn't a little chicken come up to me in the dust and kneel down begging me to stay?
p.d	I'm not afraid of being on my own
abe	You're very lucky
p.d	I've been like it since the day I was born
abe	It's strange how lucky some people are
p.d	(SUDDENLY LOOKS AT HIM) We've been through so much together

abe	Have we? Wait. There's a strange sweetness in the air. What is this taste in my mouth?
p.d	GETS UP
abe	Where are you going?
	A LORRY APPROACHES WITH A WHINING WHEEL
p.d	I'll get a lift on my own
abe	I'll come with you
p.d	It'll be quicker with just one
abe	I dare say
p.d	Bye
p.d	GOES
abe	(QUIETLY, NOT CALLING) Come back. Strange girl
	PAUSE
	(CALLS OUT) My washing! I suppose I'll have to take it down myself. Haven't I given you my all?
	GETS UP. SHIVERS
	Embers of the fire, what shall I do now? The girl has left me.
	What a long decade it has been.
	I need a job. I need a wife. I need a home!
	I'd better get cracking or this could go on for ever.
	HE TAKES DOWN HIS DRYING SUIT AND WRINGS OUT THE RAINWATER
	HE DROPS THE CLOTHES INTO THE MUD
	Where's my tin whistle?
	Where is my comb?
	Where is my framed photograph?
	(HE PICKS UP HIS CLOTHES) My clothes are covered in mud.
	(HUGS THEM TO HIM) The whole roadside is awash with mud. It's a sea of mud. Ship ahoy! (HE STICKS HIS THUMB UP TO A LORRY PASSING A LONG WAY OFF)
	Didn't I give you my all?

75

HE DRESSES IN HIS WET MUDDY SUIT AND SHIRT

(CALLS OUT) Don't you think I need the things you need?

My all was not a lot to give.

My all was not a lot to give.

It's cold. Is there anyone out there? I have the falling sickness (FALLS) My eyes. Can't anyone come forward? I'm growing weak. The sugar in my blood, it isn't enough! A Mars Bar; someone please help (HE STRUGGLES IN THE MUD, HOLDING HIS HEAD) Mamma, Mamma

p.d	COMES BACK
p.d	Look what I found
abe	(FROM THE MUD) Mud ...
p.d	A suitcase
abe	Muddy, mud ...
p.d	It's empty
abe	I'm not a well man
p.d	What is it?
abe	Well, my father died of sclerosis of the liver
p.d	Oh
abe	I can't remember it it's hereditary
p.d	STRAIGHTENS HER SLEEVE
abe	I'm sorry you should find me like this
p.d	TUCKS HER HAIR BEHIND HER EAR
abe	(STILL GROPING IN THE MUD) You can see what a wild rover I would have been if it wasn't for this infirmity I have. Muddy, mud ...
p.d	Listen shall I help you up or something?
abe	You're hardly up to it
p.d	Here (PUTS OUT HER ARM)
abe	Can we not head off this awful moment in some other way. Let me turn on my back so I can see you. We can talk
p.d	I have to go

abe	You've only just arrived
p.d	My mother will be wondering where I am
abe	I remember the name
p.d	My mother
abe	Your mother?
p.d	My mother will be wondering where I am
abe	Yes, I remember. Well, thanks for all your help in washing my clothes. Unfortunately they're dirty again. You should have seen me on my wedding day

A LORRY WITH A WHINING WHEEL TRAVELS PAST

A lorry. It's wheel was whining

What a marvellous landscape

p.d	I think we'll be friends for ever
abe	You say the nicest things
p.d	I like you very much and I hope you will always be my friend
abe	Yes surely. I'll write you a letter. oh no, I forgot, you've already been getting my letters to my wife. I know, you just keep on reading those. I'll hold you in mind while I write them in future
p.d	I think one day we'll, we'll be a great pair together and people will talk about us in the same breath always ...
abe	What a wonderful future you have planned for us. I only hope we run into each other sometimes so it can all come true
p.d	Bye (GOES)
abe	Yes goodbye (LIES BACK IN THE MUD)

How can I forget that smell.

I wonder will she come back again? We could take the road together. She promised eternal friendship.

What a wonderful thing. I've got to get moving.

Hunger and Cold. Hunger and Cold

★ ★ ★

ABE AND THE DARK WOMAN, ROLL OUT ONTO THE BALCONY TOGETHER.
SHE HAS HER BRIDAL VEIL ON HER HEAD

dark woman   What are you doing here anyway?

abe   I found myself here

dark woman   (INAUDIBLY) Get out of my house

abe   This! This spot is the meeting place of everyone thrown out of here!
Here give me your hand. Who brought you here?
Those years ago. Recount for me now

dark woman   I fought my way in by myself you fool. For all the help you were I might as well have stayed put. They didn't want women of my race here for hear we'd light fires. But I showed them

abe   Ah, you swept me off my feet

dark woman   And from that very day they haven't left me a moment's peace. Why didn't you keep them from me

abe   If you must know, I followed my little babbies around from a distance where they couldn't see me. And in this four cornered world I tried to keep them from harm

dark woman   Oh, is that it?

abe   It is my true story

dark woman   Oh, and I'll tell you mine. With the first baby born they came and pulled the blankets from the windows and pulled off the door, with the second came the summons for arrears of rent, with the third they came and put barbed wire around our garden, with little Kerry number four they said they'd burn me if there were any more, with number five they took away the steel and iron you'd left rotting here - You'd better get out lassie and take your brood with you, God rot them! - and with number six they chased me away and before number seven they had chased me back again and wouldn't let me go

And if you were looking for them how come you never found them?

abe	Never found them? Oh but the roads were long, very, very long. I'd no idea where even to start
dark woman	You've no cunning. I come from a line of cunning men. You fell for their tricks all along, didn't you?
abe	I did, I did. They told me - If yous can get a house fit to live in you can have your kiddies back. But when I went to ask for a house do you know what they said? If you can get your kiddies back you can have a house
	Oh, if they'd rolled the Earth as flat as they've rolled you and me, we'd have fallen off the edge of it long ago
dark woman	Go away from me now. You stink the stink of loneliness. You're desperate about every minute and every night, aren't you! Well, I'm not. I think of it year by year, and I've never fallen to my knees in the small hours in front of the mirror and asked - who, who, who will speak to me? -
abe	(LOOKING OVER THE BALCONY RAIL AT THE WORLD) Yes, I know, I hate to leave you though. Can you manage in the dark with the wheelchair and the stairs, isn't it very difficult? I would stay and help you
dark woman	What? And have them catch you here in the morning?
abe	Well, if you do see one of the babbies, take him in
dark woman	You don't need to tell me that. And if you see one?
abe	If it's a boy give him a kick, if it's a girl give her a milk stout
	HE SMILES AT HER, SHE LAUGHS

★   ★   ★

ABE IS AT THE ROADSIDE, P.D COMES BACK

abe	Are you still here?
	Haven't you got a home to go to?
p.d	Of course I have
abe	You could introduce me to all your friends
p.d	They've all gone
abe	I expect they are busy with their jobs

p.d	Yes
abe	(PAUSE) Maybe they will want to help us?
p.d	Who?
abe	Help me up then and we'll carry on by ourselves. Guided by our own pure thoughts we'll think of one thing and one thing only
p.d	What?
abe	It doesn't matter, God will inform us

SHE HELPS HIM UP

We'll earn money. We'll meet lots of people.
We'll get everyone, bring them all with us

p.d	Don't you want me for yourself?
abe	Ah this time of day! It's a Sunday, hot and dusty, the empty motorway stretches out ahead of us in the heat. So peaceful. That way lies America, the great unknown continent, and that way sober Asia with her undiscovered vale of tears. To the south, Africa, my brothers and sisters grinding two solitary grains on a stone, their caravans are coming this way ...
p.d	Don't you want me for yourself?
abe	Oh if only you didn't need money to travel I would be a nomad myself
p.d	I don't feel well
abe	No, you feel alright don't you?
p.d	I'm ill
abe	What do you need?
p.d	MOANS GENTLY
abe	I know a man. If we go to him tomorrow he can get you access to a hospital bed
p.d	No (MOANS)
abe	Is there nothing I can give you? I know, we can walk to the sea. Eastbourne. You'd love it. I know a couple of nurses there, they said I was very avante-garde (HE LAUGHS FONDLY)
p.d	Oh! (SHE GROANS)

abe	Where's your ma?
p.d	She remarried
abe	Oh my poor darling!
p.d	Are you falling in love with me?
abe	It's difficult to love the sick -
p.d	Aren't you
abe	- except to learn to minister the suffering Christ in them
p.d	(HOLDING HER STOMACH) Can't you love me?
abe	Can you be the suffering Christ?
p.d	I'm not well enough

FALLS TO HER KNEES AND WOULD BE SICK BUT SHE LACKS THE STRENGTH

abe	Ah well, it's a long road, We'd better get started
p.d	(FEVERISH, WEAK, ON THE GROUND) No, no
abe	And when night comes the dogs will bark, the shutters come down, and you and I, ... and everything will - ... you and I, we - ... you - ...

HE LOOKS DOWN AT HER

Are you ill? Shall I help you?

p.d	Help me!
abe	When I think of all the friends I've known who have gone down in this way. I remember even on my wedding day, my companions fell into the gutter like ashes into a pool ...

IT HAS BECOME DUSK, THE SKY IS CLEAR AND DARKENING, A PALE TINT AT ITS EDGE

Do you need water? We haven't any

HE TAKES OFF HIS COAT

p.d	I need water!
abe	Here, have my coat (HE LAYS IT OVER HER)

A DOG BARKS

NIGHT FALLS

★   ★   ★

ABE IS STANDING BELOW THE BALCONY

abe   Madam! Madam! I know you're in there! I want a word! Stop your hiding!

P.D APPEARS ON THE BALCONY, HER HAIR FLOWING AND SHINING, WELL BRUSHED; HER LIPS LIKE CHERRIES, HER EYES SPARKLING; BUT ANY LOOK OF HEALTH HAS FINALLY DISAPPEARED

p.d   What do you want?

abe   Please be so good as to get me your mistress

p.d   My what?

abe   Your employer

p.d   My what?

abe   Your mother, get her down here

p.d   My what?

abe   Your friend

p.d   Listen

abe   I look like this because of the way I live. It's a very traditional culture

p.d   Listen, fuck it

abe   It's a tradition of suffering and persecution. It's becoming very fashionable now you'll find

p.d   Please don't

abe   Look at my jewellery. My rings. Hand made. Stolen

p.d   GOES IN

abe   Come on

ABE TAKES OUT SOME MUD FROM HIS JACKET POCKET AND THROWS IT AT THE WINDOW

p.d   REAPPEARS

abe   Hello there. I wonder if I could have a word?

p.d   Go on then

abe   It's like this; I'm a born loser otherwise I'd ask you to come down and sort it out with blows

p.d	Is that it?
abe	You must be very busy
p.d	Yes ...
abe	The only thing is, the rent is going up
p.d	What?
abe	The rent. Up. It goes as from today
p.d	So what?
abe	Also -
p.d	So what? Because she doesn't pay it anyway
abe	One more thing. We're repossessing the property
p.d	What?
abe	And then selling it
p.d	So what's the point of putting the rent up?
abe	We want to cover all the exits
p.d	The what?
abe	Exits. The exits. Cover all the exits. We want to -
p.d	Yeah
abe	So
p.d	So what?
abe	So if you tell her I'd like a word

THE DARK WOMAN WHEELS ONTO THE BALCONY

dark woman	What is it honey?
p.d	Nothing, it's nothing
abe	It's me (PAUSE) I had an errand but I've forgotten it now
dark woman	Oh. Well, what are you trying to do?
abe	I came -
dark woman	What's the point? Can't you see I can manage by myself
abe	Yes, it's true
dark woman	I brought up your children, you never helped
abe	I was on the high seas

dark woman	No you weren't
abe	If the social security had paid up I might have settled down
dark woman	My life counted for nothing. My whole life you wasted
abe	Just now, I was occupied momentarily. A young girl, barely literate but a great wit, tried to seduce me by spilling her bodily fluids on me. I resisted but she eclipsed my whole personality with her darkness.
	Come away with me now and we'll lead a gay old life. I thought we could live on the land. I have a piece in mind. I brought some of it here in my pocket, look
dark woman	Leave me be
abe	But what is left in store? Your children are gone. You have no home, no money, your health is failing. Bleak years ahead
dark woman	You want my house for yourself! That's it isn't it!
abe	No, no. What would I gain from your moving away? You're the only person I know on this earth
dark woman	You'd enjoy the thrill of being totally alone
abe	No, no woman!
p.d	APPEARS BELOW WITH HER SUITCASE
abe	Another thing is, I think I may be going blind. I need someone to lead me about
dark woman	That is a very selfish thing
abe	As you well know invalids must be iron willed. You and I could go forth together up the A1. You have kith and kin residing on its banks. We can go and find them, they'll give us succour I know
p.d	Go with him, I don't care
dark woman	I'll not go with him, you go with him
p.d	I'm not going with him
dark woman	I'm not leaving this house
p.d	I don't want your house if that's what you're thinking

abe	Go inside child
p.d	I'm not going inside, you go inside
abe	I'm a little too old to go acting on advice
p.d	(TO DARK WOMAN) Why don't you take what you're given. What's wrong with unhappiness. People should be unhappy. It's good for them
abe	Your constant blessing, day in, day out, it's like a curse -
p.d	Especially children. Look at me, I don't regret anything. When I was a child -
abe	She's still only a child
p.d	I had to lay in wait like a fox for my dinner ...
abe	(TO DARK WOMAN) I ... I ... Have no stronger argument
p.d	(SHE SWAYS) But at least I'm alive ... I'm glad -
abe	(SPITS) God forgive me my ignorance
dark woman	God damn your ignorance!
abe	Look, some children in pushchairs being trundled past. God, isn't that a sight!
	Hello Micky Mouse! Hello! Hello!
dark woman	Get away form me, leave us
p.d	No, don't say that to him!
abe	She's right. What's done is done and the future's never far behind
p.d	(PICKS UP HER SUITCASE) Help me with this
abe	(PICKS UP THE SUITCASE) This doesn't weigh a thing
p.d	Just carry it a little way for me, that's it. Here, here come on
dark woman	You and your tricks
p.d	I have a right!
dark woman	You have no right, you're just a child, leave him alone
p.d	Just carry it to the corner for me and I'll wait for the bus
dark woman	Oh a bus now is it? Why don't you hop in a taxi? She's a little

grand now isn't she!

p.d   I am grand! I'm going to be grand. I'm alive, and ... all my grandness and ... my body ... my whole body ... People will kiss me

abe   God bless the little one! You see Mary, you should learn that -

dark woman   Wake up now Dermot

abe   I am awake. Are you in pain?

dark woman   Only my eyes

abe   Who are you weeping for?

★   ★   ★

P.D APPEARS ON THE BALCONY, HER HAIR FLOWING AND SHINING, WELL BRUSHED; HER LIPS LIKE CHERRIES, HER EYES SPARKLING; BUT ANY LOOK OF HEALTH HAS FINALLY DISAPPEARED

abe   I look like this because of the way I live. It's a very traditional culture

p.d   Listen -

abe   It's a tradition of suffering and persecution. It's becoming very fashionable now you'll find. It's like this; I'm a born loser otherwise -

p.d   Is that it?

abe   I'd like a word

p.d   We're very busy

abe   I know you are, Many have tried to steal her. I've let them. I stood by. Where is my stolen wife? Poor woman!

p.d   Your wife?

abe   My wife. My friend. My mistress

p.d   She won't come out. Because they're repossessing the property. She's hiding

abe   So what? (HE STAGGERS TOWARDS THE DOORWAY AND THUMPS ON THE DOOR) Please, please! Mrs James! (HE IS TEARFUL) There's a man here to see you!

Mrs James!

THE DARK WOMAN COMES ONTO THE BALCONY

dark woman	(TO P.D) What is it honey?
p.d	He's come about the rent
abe	She has the proper air of the business woman doesn't she?
dark woman	Leave her alone
abe	She was the lonely child of the roadway when I knew her
p.d	(TO ABE) Look what I've got here
abe	What is it but an empty suitcase?

P.D GOES IN

abe	Another thing is, I think I may be going blind. I need someone to lead me about
dark woman	That's a very selfish thing
abe	Well as you know, invalids must be iron willed. The alternative is oblivion

P.D COMES BACK OUT

p.d	No, you're wrong, it's something else!
abe	You and I could go forth together up the A1. You have kith and kin residing on its banks. We can go and find them, they'll give us succour I know
dark woman	I've had enough of your blab

P.D COMES FORWARD

p.d	Abe, look inside
abe	No, wait a minute -
p.d	I lost the ugly duckling!
abe	Isn't that what you wanted to happen?
p.d	Yes but ... Oh Abe! Hey do you want to see it?
abe	What? (HE LOOKS UP FOR THE DARK WOMAN BUT SHE IS NOT THERE)
p.d	I've got it here, I put it in this suitcase
abe	You did?

p.d	Yes I brought it here to you
abe	To me? But Lord, I don't want it!
p.d	(IN TEARS) No, no but -
	SHE PULLS BACK HER TEARS, PUTS HER HAIR BEHIND HERS EARS AND STRAIGHTENS HER SLEEVE
	No, no wait until you see it. It's really nice. Sweet little thing
abe	Stop it. Keep it away from me!
p.d	(OPENS SUITCASE) Wait till you see it ...
abe	I don't want to see it!
p.d	Why not?
abe	It's a terrible thing to -
p.d	But it's part of me!
abe	It's not a part of you!
p.d	But who is it a part of then?
abe	No one! It's not a part of anyone!
p.d	But it was growing in my body!
abe	Listen ...
p.d	It's me!
abe	No!
p.d	Here you see (THOROUGHLY DEFEATED SHE NEVERTHELESS TRIES TO PRESENT THE SUITCASE TO HIM)
abe	No! (AWKWARDLY HE BOOTS THE SUITCASE AWAY)
	THE DARK WOMAN APPEARS AT THE DOORWAY, STANDING.
	P.D PICKS UP THE DROPPED SUITCASE, SHE PEEPS AT WHAT'S INSIDE RESTORING THE DISTURBED CONTENTS WITH HER HAND
p.d	No, I - (SHE STUMBLES WITH THE SUITCASE)
abe	I'm sorry child
p.d	SMILES AWKWARDLY
dark woman	Wake up now Dermot
abe	I am awake

dark woman	Are you in pain?
abe	Only my eyes
dark woman	Poor Abe!
abe	Don't weep for me, weep for yourselves
p.d	Would he like to rest his head on my suitcase?
dark woman	Possibly

P.D SHOVES THE SUITCASE UNDER HIS HEAD

THE END

First performed at Liverpool Playhouse Studio in March 1993

A Message for the Broken Hearted

SITTING ON A BENCH IN A GARDEN

linda   Mickey ... do you think there's anything wrong with our relationship?

mickey   (SMILES IRONICALLY)

linda   What's wrong do you think?

mickey   Out of chaos came disaster, then out of disaster came chaos, then out of chaos came disaster

linda   Oh. Don't you think it's because you're having an affair with Jenine?

mickey   No

    (THEY EAT THEIR ICE LOLLIES. SHE LICKS AROUND HERS WITH A LONG SEDUCTIVE TONGUE, THEN BITES OFF ABRUBPTLY)

linda   I make you feel lonely, don't I?

mickey   Yes

linda   (SHE LOOKS AT HIM WITH A VAST RANGE OF SUPPRESSED FEELINGS PASSING ACROSS HER FACE. SHE LOOKS DOWN, HER EYES ARE FULL OF A DISHONEST HATRED SHE IS UNAWARE OF)

    Sorry (SHE DOESN'T MEAN IT BUT SHE THINKS SHE DOES)

mickey   That's ok

linda   I just don't like it when you think I'm abnormal

mickey   How do you know I think you're abnormal

linda   Because I am. But if you were nice to me I'd be better

mickey   I am nice to you

linda   Never for long enough

mickey   Because you're never better for long enough

    (PAUSE)

linda   Tell me you love me

mickey   (HE TURNS TO HER. OPENS HIS MOUTH, MAKES A SERIES OF DREADFUL GRIMACES BUT CAN MAKE NO WORDS COME OUT. HE COLLAPSES IN A FAINT. SHE LOOKS DOWN AT HIM)

linda	It's alright for you, you've got somewhere else to go. I've got nothing. I'm all alone in a black pit of despair
mickey	(ON THE GROUND, DOESN'T MOVE. OPENS ONE EYE) You've got your father
linda	My father is darkness
mickey	I've dropped my mivvi
linda	Have mine
mickey	Thanks. (DOESN'T MOVE)
linda	Do you remember when we met?
mickey	Yep. (SITS UP. TAKES HER ICE-LOLLY)
linda	I was lovely
mickey	Yes, you were
linda	And still only a child. How you loved me then!
mickey	I still -
linda	What?
mickey	I still -
linda	Mickey, you're eating my mivvi
mickey	I said, I still -
linda	Mickey, there's a spider on your face
mickey	It's a moth
linda	Why do you blame me for everything that's gone wrong
mickey	Because it's all your fault
linda	Yes, you say that but I'm not sure I can believe it
mickey	You can't believe it? Well who's fault do you think it is then. Mine?
linda	Nno, no not yours - I didn't say that did I?
mickey	Don't look at me like that
linda	(STARES AT HIM)
mickey	Did you hear me?
linda	Yes

mickey	Stop it
linda	(SHE SHRINKS FROM HIM)
mickey	(HE SHRINKS FROM HER IN IMITATION. THEN RUSHES BACK AT HER) Don't shrink from me like that
linda	(STARING) I didn't
mickey	You didn't
	(MR STEVENSON COMES OUT OF THE HOUSE)
mr stevenson	Unhand my daughter this instant
mickey	Oh it's you. Why don't you do something about your daughter
mr stevenson	Don't you think I've tried? Sometimes I think if I had strength left in these hands I'd strangle the last breath out of her
mickey	What do you want out here? Why don't you go back to your ..... and leave us alone
mr stevenson	I came to ask how long you intend to live in this house. The overcrowding is affecting my asthma
mickey	Not a moment longer
mr stevenson	Oh yes and where will you go, you're penniless. When I was your age, I had a string of attractive women to receive me
mickey	What makes you think I don't, eh?
mr stevenson	Your obvious relish for my daughter is proof enough. Why can't you find yourself a normal, healthy woman
mickey	I've never met one
mr stevenson	Misogynist! You'll never touch my daughter again. What is this sticky mess I'm standing in?
mickey	That's my ice-lolly
mr stevenson	Thank god. I thought it was one of Linda's calamities. Come inside for Christ's sake before the neighbours see us

★   ★   ★

A ROOM, DARKNESS. PERSISTENT KNOCKING ON THE DOOR. STOPS. PERSISTENT KNOCKING ON THE WINDOW. HUSHED VOICES INSIDE THE ROOM

mickey	Open it

jenine	I'm not opening it

SOUND OF A PIECE OF COAT HANGER SCRAPING AROUND THE WINDOW, ITSELF BEHIND DRAWN CURTAINS

mickey	She's trying to open the window
jenine	What shall we do?
mickey	Don't move or she'll see you
jenine	She's gone mad out there. Oh why didn't we open it?
mickey	It's too late now, here she comes

AS THE WINDOW IS FINALLY FORCED OPEN A FEMALE FIGURE LEAPS FROM A BED AND SCAMPERS ACROSS THE ROOM IN HER UNDERWEAR, AND OUT. THE CURTAINS ARE SUDDENLY TORN DOWN AND ANOTHER FEMALE FIGURE EMERGES THROUGH THE WINDOW, LINDA

linda	That's charming. (STEPS ONTO A SOFA THEN ONTO THE FLOOR, TURNS THE LIGHT ON)
mickey	(SITTING ON THE BED WRAPPED IN A BLANKET) Hello
linda	Where is she?
mickey	Who?

(JENINE RE-ENTERS IN HER KNICKERS)

jenine	Hello Linda
linda	Thanks. (TO JENINE) Are you pregnant?
jenine	No
linda	Why not?
jenine	Because I'm not allowed to be
linda	So ... Well I must say it feels different to actually see it
mickey	Where are my trousers?
linda	... it makes me feel ill
mickey	... under the chair
linda	... a bit sick
mickey	You always feel sick, twenty four hours a day
linda	It's a nervous complaint, Mickey

mickey	Hand them to me Jenine
jenine	Get them yourself
linda	I know what's going on now, don't I?
jenine	Really? I wish you'd tell me
linda	Mickey knows ... come on explain
mickey	... I spend the whole time explaining
linda	... light-hearted, aren't I?
mickey	... in fact it's so long since I had an honest thought in my head ...
linda	This won't do you any good
jenine	(PUTS HER COAT ON) You'll be torn in two forever
linda	You'll end up with neither
jenine	You'll be lonely
linda	Leave her
jenine	Leave her
mickey	Yes
linda	Which?
mickey	Yes, whichever
linda	If you have a child with her, you'll ruin my life
mickey	(TO JENINE) There, you see it's not possible
jenine	A whole side of me has opened up like a trap, it's too late
mickey	Linda your shoes are digging into my trousers. If you lift your heel you will flick them over here to me
jenine	... and when you two have children, where will that leave me?
mickey	Where?
jenine	Standing in the kitchen in my knickers as always ... I don't know why I'm hanging around
linda	No why are you?
jenine	I suppose I'm hoping for my own good as well as his that he'll change his mind. (PICKS UP THE PHONE) Can I use it? I have to pick up Wilberforce from nursery

linda	Why not? Go on
jenine	After all, you were always talking long distance on mine
linda	That was because I wasn't well
jenine	And now I can't pay my bill
linda	Well? I'm sorry. (TO MICKEY) How do you think it feels to be called into question like this?
jenine	Hello. Can I have a cab please, same address, yes. If it's cut off, I'll be isolated from all my friends because of you
mickey	She needs friends, Linda. Why did you do that?
linda	(NOT ANSWERING) It hurts
jenine	You see, you'll be left with nothing. Make up your mind, I don't mind if it's her
mickey	Would someone give me my trousers
jenine	Poor linda. I love her too but I can still see what a terrible waste it all is. All we ever hear about is this fairytale romance and even I have been in love with it but now I'm sick of it. She gives you nothing and I'm bursting with so much I could give you, all you need but I won't ever be able to because I am second best and always have been
mickey	It's not like that. I love you, I love her
jenine	You're driving me mad like you've driven her mad
micky	Judas
jenine	I know nothing is harder than to give her up but in losing the most you would gain the most. Nothing is easier than giving me up but in losing the least you will gain the least ... why am I saying this?
mickey	Why are you saying this?
jenine	Because I love you
linda	This has got to stop
mickey	I agree
linda	I'm beginning to realise how much damage all this has done to me
jenine	I'm going, goodbye Linda

linda	(TEARS) Goodbye
jenine	If it's any consolation, I'm going to hurt more than anyone because I'm the odd one out. (THEY EMBRACE THEN JENINE BREAKS FROM LINDA AND MOVES TO GO) I want you to sell your motorbike
mickey	Why?
jenine	You know why
linda	Why?
jenine	Please Mickey, sell it, don't prevaricate, it would be cruel. I couldn't bear to think of you riding about on it without me. Goodbye
mickey	Sell it, yes, anything
jenine	You can phone me if you need me, otherwise don't. (GOES OUT)
	LINDA WALKS OUT AND AWAY, HANDS DANGLING BY HER SIDES, LEAVING MICKEY STANDING ALONE. HE PUTS HIS TROUSERS ON AND PUTS HIS HAND OVER HIS EYES LIKE A VISOR, THE OTHER HAND OVER HIS EAR AND STUMBLES ABOUT BLINDLY. JENINE COMES BACK INTO THE ROOM, MICKEY STARES AT HER
jenine	What?
mickey	What?
jenine	Leave me alone, will you please. You do understand that? Otherwise I'll be stuck like this forever ...(PAUSE)
mickey	Are you going to wait out there?
jenine	For a little while, until the taxi comes. What are you going to do?
mickey	(SHRUGS)
jenine	Tell her you can't live without me
mickey	Yes, ok
jenine	Don't do it because I tell you
mickey	No ...
jenine	Do it because ... (PAUSE) ... kiss me goodbye then
	MICKEY KISSES HER, FALLS SLEEPILY INTO HER ARMS
jenine	Don't go to sleep

★   ★   ★

A TAXI ARRIVES, DOOR OPENS, CLOSES. TAXI DEPARTS

A FEW MOMENTS LATER JENINE WALKS SLOWLY INTO VIEW IN FRONT OF THE HOUSE DRESSED IN A SMART JACKET WITH A NEAT SKIRT SPLIT UP THE SIDE, HAT, GLOVES AND HANDBAG. SHE WALKS UP THE STEPS TO THE DOOR BUT CHANGES HER MIND COMES DOWN AND SITS SEDATELY ON A GARDEN CHAIR, WAITS

MICKEY COMES OUT RUBBING HIS EYES, STUMBLES AND NEARLY FALLS DOWN THE STEPS

jenine   Did you tell her I was coming?

mickey   Why don't you go in and say hello?

jenine   Who to?

mickey   I don't know, maybe the children will recognise you

jenine   Is the taxi still there?

mickey   Go and look

JENINE   (STANDS UP AND GOES OUT)

MICKEY PICKS UP THE CHAIR SHE WAS SITTING ON AND TRIES TO SMASH IT AGAINST THE WALL, THROWS CHAIR AWAY

LINDA COMES OUT GASPING FOR BREATH

linda   For God's sake! Help me, Mickey! I can't get enough air indoors, quick, help me sit down. Where's that garden chair?

mickey   I don't know

linda   You've probably smashed it up. Go and find it

MICKEY TAKES A FEW BLIND STEPS IN NO DIRECTION

LINDA SEES JENINE WHO RE-ENTERS. LINDA COMPOSES HER SELF

linda   Beautiful this place of mine, isn't it? (SIGHS)

MICKEY RETURNS TO LINDA AFTER STAGGERING IN A CIRCLE

linda   (TO JENINE) Have you seen my chair?

jenine   Mickey call another taxi

mickey   Call one yourself

linda   (DISTRESSED) My chair

100

jenine	Where are my bags?
linda	Have you lost something?
jenine	Yes, my luggage
linda	Mickey, find Jenine's luggage
mickey	The taxi drove off with it
jenine	Mickey, I'm leaving. Call a taxi
mickey	(IGNORES THE ORDER) Bye bye, Linda love
linda	Bye Mickey. Jenine's confused, Mickey
jenine	Why are you here, Linda?
linda	I got the days muddled up. What are you here for? I think it's tragic the way your friendship is going to be sacrificed for all this ... where are you going?
jenine	Where, Mickey?
mickey	We're going to the the
linda	to the ... ??
mickey	Linda, shut up, shut up. Mind your own business
linda	Jenine, do you want to go dancing, tomorrow?
jenine	With you?
linda	Yes, dancing. (SHE DEMONSTRATES)
mickey	Linda, could you go inside
linda	(SHE GOES UP THE STEPS) Alright, Mickey
jenine	Yes, I'd like to
linda	Alright then. (AS SHE GOES IN)
mickey	(PAUSE) Who was that on the swing, just now?
jenine	(GOES OVER TO THE SWING) I was
	A BABY STARTS CRYING INSIDE THE HOUSE. LINDA COMES OUT AIMLESSLY DOWN THE STEPS. PAUSE. THEY ALL STARE AT EACH OTHER
linda	Mickey, do you know why the baby is crying?
jenine	Christ ...
mickey	Is it?

linda	(TO MICKEY) What's the matter?
mickey	Is the baby crying?
jenine	Linda
linda	Yes?
jenine	What's the matter darling?
linda	Mickey, would you?
mickey	No
linda	Jenine, where's your baggage?
jenine	In the taxi, apparently
linda	Stop that fucking baby!
mickey	(BLIND) Where is it?
linda	Indoors! It's indoors somewhere!
mickey	Point me at the steps
jenine	What are you doing, Mickey, stop it!
mickey	Linda, help me, I can't see
jenine	Of course he can
mickey	Linda, help me
linda	What's wrong with him?
jenine	Mickey

MICKEY FALLS ON HIS FACE. DOESN'T MOVE

jenine	Mickey, I'm going
mickey	No ...
jenine	Yes, listen, I'll come and visit you
mickey	No, don't leave me here
linda	What's the matter? Mickey, you're so ... oh I don't know
mickey	Tell her to stop, I'm not well
jenine	You're fine, stand up
mickey	Please don't
linda	Don't touch him, Jenine

jenine	But Linda
linda	No, because you know why, I caught you together, didn't I? So don't touch him
jenine	(GETS UP, STEPS BACK) Alright
linda	Do you think it strange my dad deals with the baby crying?
jenine	Lovely. I don't care
linda	Why not?
jenine	It's not my baby
linda	But you'd like it to be?
mickey	Linda, I think I know where your chair is
linda	Don't start that Mickey now
mickey	Christ knows we all need a sit down every now and again
linda	You might
mickey	I do, yes
jenine	Can you dance, Linda?
linda	Yes, I'm very sexy
mickey	- except she's got little piggy eyes
linda	You can't see my eyes because I close them
mickey	Shifty pools of piss
linda	Don't spoil it Mickey
mickey	It gives me the creeps just looking at you
linda	What's the matter with me?
mickey	I think it must be your body language, love ...
linda	Oh
mickey	... reminds me of a trip to the cemetery
linda	Oh ...
mickey	... that and your face ...
linda	... anything else?
mickey	... nothing, except you bore me rigid

linda	... I know ...
mickey	... and everyone else
linda	I don't think so
mickey	Ask anyone, if you can keep their attention long enough
linda	(TO JENINE) He's so rude, isn't he?
jenine	I'm just a weapon between you, aren't I Mickey?
mickey	Look at her
jenine	(LOOKS AT LINDA)
linda	(LOOKS AT JENINE, A WEAK SMILE ENDEAVOURING TO HIDE HER ANGER)
mickey	Who wants to be looked at like that?
jenine	Let's arrange another day
mickey	Do you want me to stay and look after you Linda?
linda	(CRIES) Yes
mickey	Alright, I'll go and get my cudgel
linda	(LOOKS AT HIM, UNCOMPREHENDING)
mickey	My cudgel, I said
linda	(STARES AT HIM, FROZEN)
mickey	(RAISES HIS FIST AT HER) My cudgel
linda	(TEARS)

JENINE TURNS AND LEAVES. LINDA AND MICKEY GO INSIDE. NIGHT FALLS, TIME PASSES

★ ★ ★

DAY BREAKS

LINDA, MICKEY AND MR STEVENSON COME OUT OF THE HOUSE INTO THE GARDEN. MR STEVENSON STANDS SUPERCILIOUSLY REGARDING HIS BORDERS

mickey	I bet he's had his finger in your pie
mr stevenson	Does he know how depressed I am Linda?
mickey	... I can see
mr stevenson	Wait until Sunday, my breath falls into the wall and my eyes weeping like a liquor still ...

mickey	I won't make it to Sunday at this rate
mr stevenson	Oh, have your lost your love?
mickey	I've lost two. They warned me ...
mr stevenson	You see, he's fallen under my charm
linda	Why are all these leaves still lying on the floor, why?
mr stevenson	Yes, they do drive us back upon our memories, don't they?
mickey	Why what?
linda	All you've done is lie to me for years, I think you've taken advantage of me
mr stevenson	Yes, you've availed yourself of her weakness, young man. Her weakness in the head, like an egg, unbroken and yet rancid inside. Oh how can I be happy? The girl cries beside me in bed at night. It's very upsetting, we're both asleep; but sleep-?

Wait until after dinner, I could thrust you all apart. All this standing staring ... you're all mad. Is there someone outside my garden? |
linda	Is she outside?
mr stevenson	(TO HIMSELF. SCRATCHING A FLEA INDIGNANTLY) What's going on ...
mickey	Who?
linda	I thought I saw her
mickey	No, I can't see anyone
linda	How long will this go on, I can't get her out of my mind

Every time I look at you, she's behind you. She hates me now, at last openly hates me, she wishes I would drown

A KNOCK AT THE GARDEN GATE |
mr stevenson	At last my taxi has arrived
linda	You're not going anywhere, Daddy. (GOES TO LOOK) It's her
mickey	Unlock the gate then, blimey
mr stevenson	Me? I wouldn't know what to say.
linda	She must be protected from all pain, while I ...

(SIGHS) |

               ... I am not to be protected. Why?

               because I'm the winner

mr stevenson My daughter? The winner? I never allowed it

linda The loser has come round to gloat

mr stevenson It must be the taxi I think, pardon me please

mickey Stop edging forward, get back

mr stevenson Don't stop me please. Youth, Ah!

> GATE OPENS. JENINE STEPS IN, SMILES AT MICKEY, STANDS BY THE GATE, OPENS HER HANDBAG
>
> SILENCE

linda What's she doing here?

mr stevenson Now, now, now, if a beautiful girl wants to mount the steps to my house ...

jenine Hello Mickey

mr stevenson Who is she? Has she come to announce something?

jenine I saw your children outside playing ...

mickey (INTERRUPTING. TO MR STEVENSON) Your taxi has arrived

mr stevenson But I'm not going anywhere

jenine (TO LINDA) Don't look at me like that. People always want what they can't have, while at the same time they destroy what they were attracted to. How are you?

linda Much better, yes much better. I'm better you know, whereas you, I can see, you're much worse. Oh you're so much worse. Nothing has helped you

jenine (BOWS HEAD POLITELY. SMILES)

linda We're rich now, money came from nowhere

jenine Yes, we're all a shade better than we used to be

linda Even Mickey

jenine Yes?

linda Have you seen the way he stumbles about though?

jenine	And does he still have a constant fever?
linda	All that shaking and gasping?
mr stevenson	Is this his lover? Her breasts are smaller than I imagined
mickey	She breast fed too long
jenine	Does he still say he's a genius?
linda	He tries to explain that to me, but I don't understand
jenine	You never listened
linda	Only because I knew you would
jenine	Every word fell like gold coins into my heart ...
linda	And now, how is your heart?
jenine	Open
linda	Isn't the world cruel
jenine	Yes, but I'm free to enjoy it
mr stevenson	I'm surprised by your appearance madam; Linda, how could you have competed with this lovely girl, she wins my heart immediately
mickey	Isn't she lovely?
mr stevenson	Do you know my dear, my heart is full of stones? My daughter won't respond to my caresses
	JENINE JUST SMILES, HOLDS HER GROUND
mr stevenson	Isn't she strong
linda	Yes, what a performance. Mickey, I don't feel very well
mickey	(HE GOES TO HER BUT MR STEVENSON STANDS IN THE WAY)
linda	Mickey
mickey	What's wrong Linda?
linda	Sickness. (SHE TURNS AWAY)
mr stevenson	Get a bowl for her then
mickey	(HOLDS OUT HIS HANDS AND SHE IS SICK INTO THEM) Jenine pass me a tissue
jenine	(STANDS MOTIONLESS)

mr stevenson	(POURS SHERRY INTO A GLASS, HANDS IT TO LINDA) And look, look what we're drinking here, Linda is used to this aren't you lovey?
jenine	What's the matter with her?
mr stevenson	It's morning sickness I think
linda	Mickey I want to go behind a tree
mickey	Hang on, one minute, just one minute
linda	Mickey
mickey	One minute, just one minute
linda	... what are you waiting for?
mickey	I don't know
jenine	Oh for god's sake
mr stevenson	Yes, it's morning sickness I think
jenine	Is she pregnant then?
mr stevenson	I don't know, is she pregnant, Mick?
mickey	Is she what?
jenine	(ANGRY) Why didn't you tell me?
mickey	She ...
jenine	That's it, that's bloody it
linda	(VOMITS)
mr stevenson	(POLITELY) Have you seen this sort of thing before?
jenine	(SITS ON A GARDEN CHAIR IN TEARS) You bastard
mickey	Don't cry. (PUTS HIS ARM AROUND HER SHOULDER AND STROKES HER HEAD) my flaxen haired angel ...
jenine	How could you let it happen before I had time to prepare myself?
linda	(FROM BEHIND A TREE) Mickey ...
mickey	Where is she?
mr stevenson	She's popped behind the tree there
	MICKEY LIMPS BLINDLY ACROSS
mr stevenson	(GOES TO SIT DOWN PAINFULLY ON A GARDEN CHAIR) Oh, oh, oh, oh, oh, oh, help me love here will you, my coxyx isn't straight, a cushion ...

jenine	(SHOVES A CUSHION UNDER WITHOUT TURNING TO LOOK)
mickey	What the hell's wrong with her?
mr stevenson	Little slut, she's always been like it. Ate nothing but spaghetti as a child, and now look at her ...
jenine	(STANDS. CLOSES HANDBAG) Right
mickey	What?
jenine	What's the matter with her, you must know
mickey	I don't know
jenine	(SHAKES HER HEAD)
linda	(WEAKLY FROM BEHIND THE TREE) Mickey
jenine	Well ...

MICKEY SITS ON CHAIR BLINDLY

mr stevenson	(STANDS UP) Oh, are you going? A shame. My daughter you know, she's very ... have you a career?
jenine	Me? No. Why don't you attend to her?
mr stevenson	(STANDING STOCK STILL, STARING AT JENINE) I will, I will as the Lord is my witness

JENINE WALKS IN SMART SHOES AND CLOTHES AWAY

mr stevenson	Goodbye my pretty

CLIP CLOP OF JENINE'S SHOES, LINDA RUSTLES FROM BEHIND THE TREE

mr stevenson	There is a bit of conflict
mickey	We're all friends
mr stevenson	Your life is rather small I note
mickey	... It's getting smaller

★   ★   ★

LINDA AND MR STEVENSON IN A ROOM

linda	(YAWNS)
mr stevenson	I don't mind you sleeping, sleep, sleep
linda	It's alright
mr stevenson	I just wish you wouldn't yawn while I'm talking

linda	You weren't talking
mr stevenson	No, God bless you
	(PAUSE)
	Watch over me tonight
linda	Yes
mr stevenson	Am I asking too much? I will take a short walk. Don't follow this time, it's unlikely I will do anything foolish. (HE STUMBLES TO THE DOOR, TRIES TO OPEN IT BUT CAN'T. HE FALLS BACK WEAKLY) No, no, I can't, you see
	(LINDA STANDS AND DRAGS HERSELF TO THE DOOR)
	You see, you open the door for me ... without you how would I ...
linda	(TRIES THE HANDLE BUT IT BREAKS OFF) It's broken
mr stevenson	... find the beauty that waits for me outside or, being alone, how would I -
	(RETURNS AND STANDS BESIDE THE MATTRESS)
	Will you sleep now?
linda	(SHE LOOKS TOWARDS THE WINDOW)
mr stevenson	Sleep now, sleep, I'm nodding off myself. these long summer evenings, no-one around, I have nothing to think of ...
	something was mine, someone ...
	never fear, I will always pause beside you ... you are my daughter
	(LINDA SLEEPS ON THE MATTRESS
	HE GOES TO THE DOOR AND RATTLES WHAT'S LEFT OF THE HANDLE)
linda	(TALKING IN HER SLEEP) Daddy, Daddy! there's someone holding onto my arm
mr stevenson	Impossible, you are sleeping so peacefully ...
linda	Let go, let go
mr stevenson	(APPROACHES THE MATTRESS) Hello, little creature, who can you be? faceless baby sitting on the end of the bed ...
linda	Daddy, it hasn't got a face

mr stevenson (GOES AND STANDS BY HER FEET) Come on little baby let me pick you up in my arms, no I never cared for you before but now, hup, heyhup. (HE LIFTS A BLACK SHAPE FROM THE END OF THE BED)

linda It won't let go. (TO THE BLACK SHAPE)

mr stevenson There, there, little baby, come to the corner with me

linda Daddy

mr stevenson We'll see the little duckies and the pond. (GOES TO THE DOOR WITH THE BLACK SHAPE IN HIS ARMS. STANDS FACING THE DOOR HE CAN'T OPEN) I can't see past my own failure

(LINDA SLEEPS PEACEFULLY)

mr stevenson (GOES BACK TO THE BED) Linda, I can't get out. I'd like to see my garden, it's so beautiful in the summer ... get up, there's strength in you yet help me

(SHE GETS UP)

and when I've gone, you can rest

MICKEY ARRIVES OUTSIDE THE BEDROOM DOOR AND RATTLES THE HANDLE

mickey Linda, let me in

mr stevenson Who is it?

mickey Open up old man

mr stevenson What for?

mickey What for, well it isn't so I can see your silly smile. I live here

mr stevenson No you don't

mickey Where's Linda?

mr stevenson She's here, she's sleep-walking at the moment, It's most inconvenient, she can't see you

(MICKEY BURSTS OPEN THE DOOR)

You see, she doesn't know you

mickey You're quite right, never mind, since she's up I'll have her bed, you keep watch

mr stevenson I can't I'm too infirm. I'm afraid of the dark. I'll have no truck with these dreams of hers. She only does it to insult me Take her off my hands

mickey	I'm not nursing your offspring mate
mr stevenson	I'm begging you. I can't bear her silent criticisms any more. We've all made mistakes but she persecutes me. I've a good few years left in me yet, I'd like to live them in peace

(PAUSE)

mickey	What a hoax
mr stevenson	You're right my boy. I won't let you lay a finger on her, I was merely hoping for a small contribution to her psychiatric bills
mickey	Forget it
mr stevenson	What were you expecting? Some charmer I'll wager to sweeten the bitter pill of your miserable life. Well my daughter I'll have you know has more infirmities than the buttons on your coat

(LINDA FALLS SLOWLY TO THE GROUND, ASLEEP)

These fainting fits for example, who better than her father to pass the pillow under her head?

mickey	(SMILES) You've got a nice little thing going
mr stevenson	You admit it?
mickey	I'll admit anything if you let me get some sleep
mr stevenson	Go ahead, try all you like. Sleep is a stranger to this room

★   ★   ★

IN THE WOODS BESIDE A LAKE

mickey	Let's pretend we're happy beside a lake somewhere. Ducks and geese migrate overhead ... the children ...

(CHILDREN'S LAUGHTER)

... are happily playing in the water

(MICKEY SITS HAPPILY ON THE GROUND, HIS SHIRT SLEEVES AND TROUSERS ROLLED UP)

child's voice off	Watch me dancing, watch me dancing!
mickey	(TO LINDA OVER BY THE BASKET) Bring over some lemonade, let's have some lemonade

(LINDA PREPARES SOME LEMONADE)

	(TO JENINE) Sit down here beside me, ooh we're such old lovers aren't we love?
jenine	(AWKWARD SILENCE)
mickey	What's wrong?
jenine	(NO REPLY)
mickey	Not that old stuff again?
jenine	(TEARS) I don't know why
mickey	Oh well, come one, come on, watch the child dancing then … (WATCHES HER FACE) you can't even manage that can you?
jenine	(SHE STARES FROZEN WITH FEAR AT WHERE THE CHILD'S VOICE COMES FROM)
mickey	Come on, you'll disappoint the kid … stop thinking about yourself, no one's watching you
linda	(CALLING FROM THE TABLE) Mickey, there's flies in the lemonade
mickey	It doesn't matter
child's voice off	Mummy, I'm falling!
jenine	Wait darling, mummy's coming (BUT SHE'S STILL FROZEN)
mickey	(TURNS AND STARES AT JENINE'S FROZEN FACE) Boo! (HE GETS UP) Linda, where's that fucking lemonade?
linda	I spilled it …
mickey	You what?
linda	No, here's some on the table. (SHE REACHES FOR A CUP)
mickey	(TURNS AGAIN TO JENINE) Please don't stand there
jenine	Mickey
mickey	Don't, with that shawl around your face, I can't see you
jenine	I'm sorry
linda	Here mickey. (GOES TO HAND HIM A CUP OF LEMONADE BUT KNOCKS IT OVER ON THE TABLE)
mickey	Mind that cup, mind it, mind it, mind it! (IN A RAGE HE TIPS THE TABLE OVER)

linda	(FREEZES)
mickey	Everything you do is so invisible, no one else can see it, but I can see it!
linda	No, mickey
mickey	Why do you keep dropping that cup?
linda	I think it's because you react in this way
mickey	Hadn't someone better fish Wilberforce out of the lake?

JENINE STANDS UP, ROOTED TO THE SPOT

MICKEY GOES OFF TO THE SIDE

LINDA HANDS JENINE SOME LEMONADE

linda	Hadn't you better go?
jenine	What?
linda	And fish out Wilberforce
jenine	Mickey's doing it, isn't he?
linda	Do you trust him?
jenine	He's the only man I would trust alone with my children

MICKEY COMES BACK

mickey	There, I've drowned the little bugger. (GOES TO THE PICNIC HAMPER)
linda	(TO JENINE) I see. (WALKS APART)
mickey	(TO JENINE, WHO WRAPS HERSELF IN HER SHAWL) I see you're not your witty intelligent self, these days
jenine	I told you it would happen, it's your own fault
mickey	(TO LINDA) I've lost her to the ravages of the mind as well. Did you bring any drumsticks?
linda	I forgot
mickey	(TO JENINE) stop crying
jenine	It's what I'm here for. Otherwise I could be in the fields under a blue sky in the sun with your baby
linda	Tell her to -
mickey	Pardon Linda. (PUTS HIS HAND UP TO HIS EAR) I can't hear you

114

linda	Tell her to shut up
jenine	If I fell into a puddle I wouldn't make a splash. if you cut out my heart and fed it to the turtle dove that circles above us, I wouldn't murmur
	LINDA VIOLENTLY TIPS THE CONTENTS OF THE HAMPER ONTO THE GROUND
	If you laid upon me and stifled me I wouldn't gasp except with love ... all this I'd give you
mickey	(PICKS OUT FOOD FROM THE MESS) You've broken all the bloody plates
jenine	If only you'd stand and, and leave your soul behind ...
mickey	(TO LINDA, SNATCHING A SMALL SANDWICH) Give me that
jenine	I'd help you build a new one, I have your soul firmly in mind, in my breasts, there's your new soul
mickey	(TO LINDA) What's the matter aren't you going to eat or something?
linda	I've lost my appetite
mickey	(TO BOTH) Excuse me is this meant to be a picnic or not?
	JENINE LOOKS AT HIM SYMPATHETICALLY, HE CATCHES HER EYE
	And some friend you are
jenine	You haven't got any friends Mickey
mickey	I've got you
jenine	I'm not a friend any more
mickey	Well
jenine	But just because it's possible to forget someone doesn't mean you ought to, does it?
	LINDA STAMPS ON SOME PLATES AND FOOD
mickey	(PUSHES HER OUT OF THE WAY) Excuse me I want the mustard. (GOES INTO A RAGE) Where is it? (IN A HYSTERICAL FRENZY HE KICKS THE REMAINS OF THE PICNIC TO PIECES)
linda	You always have to be angrier than me
mickey	(FEROCIOUS) What?
linda	(INTIMIDATED) You -

mickey	I'm not angry, I'm looking for the bloody mustard. (HE SETS OFF ONE HAND OVER HIS EYES THE OTHER HELD TO HIS EAR)
linda	Where are you going?
mickey	For a ride
linda	When will you be back?
mickey	Soon
jenine	Are you going on your motorbike?
mickey	Yes
jenine	I thought you were selling it?
mickey	I am
jenine	When?
mickey	Soon, now if you like, just let me know
jenine	I'm jealous, I'm hurt
mickey	So am I
jenine	I can't sleep
mickey	Neither can I
linda	Neither can I
mickey	We'll all be fine
jenine	Can't you walk instead?
mickey	Would you like to come on the back?
linda	You two can't go off together like that
jenine	Those days are gone Mickey, don't you understand?
mickey	(TO LINDA) You come then
jenine	Mickey!
mickey	Alright I'll go on my own
jenine	Sell it
mickey	It's as good as sold. Where's my helmet?
	MICKEY WANDERS OFF
jenine	(TO LINDA) Love is like a poison isn't it?
linda	What?

★   ★   ★

A PARK, DUCKS, A POND NEARBY

THE WIND BLOWS, WHISTLES SADLY

MICKEY WANDERS INTO VIEW. HE WEARS A PLASTIC VISOR ABOVE HIS EYES, JEANS, TRAINERS AND A BEGRIMED ANORAK-LIKE WAIST COAT WITH THE STARS AND STRIPES PATTERN ON IT. HE CARRIES A PLASTIC BAG WITH CONTENTS

mickey	(LOOKING AROUND IN THE DISTANCE) Who's here?

HE APPROACHES A MOUND OF DAMP CLOTHES LYING ON THE GRASS

Why are you left? Where is your house, you had a house. (HE MOVES THE CLOTHES WITH HIS FOOT)

HE SETS OFF AGAIN, A SHADOW OF A MAN WALKS ACROSS THE WALL, A SMALL DOG FOLLOWS HIM ON A LEAD, HE RECEDES INTO THE DISTANCE SHRINKING

LINDA RUNS UP THE GREEN HILL AFTER HIM, STUMBLING IN HER HIGH HEELS

linda	Mickey!

HE DOESN'T TURN ROUND

Mickey (SHE STARTS CRYING) don't go!

mickey	(MICKEY TURNS AND HIDES HIS PLASTIC BAG) I'm not
linda	Don't leave me
mickey	I'm only going for a walk
linda	No, Mickey Mickey, I love you! (SHE RUNS UP TO HIM HER FACE RED AND SWELLING WITH TEARS) My lovely boy, I can't believe it! What's happening?
mickey	I don't know
linda	It's like a nightmare, help me!
mickey	I can't
linda	It's all just gone, I'm empty like a shell, take me with you
mickey	(LAUGHS) I can't very well do that can I love?

THEY LAUGH, SHE CRIES

mickey	Please

linda	Is this the moment then?
mickey	Yes...
linda	No.. (SHE REACHES OUT TO HIM)
mickey	(SHAKES HIS HEAD, ALMOST SHRUGS HIS SHOULDERS, TURNS)
linda	No! (CRIES)
mickey	(TURNS BACK) What?
linda	Where will you go?

HE WALKS

MR STEVENSON APPEARS

linda   Wait, Mickey, here's Dad

MR STEVENSON COMES

Dad look there's Mickey

mr stevenson Hello Mick

MICKEY KEEPS GOING

linda   (CATCHES MICKEY, BRINGS HIM BACK) Here's Mickey Dad

mr stevenson Hello Mick.. What's wrong with Mickey Linda?

linda   He's leaving me Dad

mr stevenson What Mick?

mickey   Yes

mr stevenson Goodbye Mick. Peter lifted up his hand like this and said: The Lord is Love

mickey   Yes

mr stevenson The Lord is Love Mickey

mickey   Yes

mr stevenson Are you leaving Linda pregnant?

mickey   (WALKS BACKWARDS, LAUGHS A BIT) Sure

mr stevenson (TO LINDA) I can't think of your mother without going into a rage... I've got to finish it, I've got to finish it I said to myself, I sat at home waiting for her, 'come home' like that 'come home' because I knew I had to finish it.. I think she was betraying me

linda	Mickey
mr stevenson	Was she do you think?
linda	Oh!
mr stevenson	Whore!
linda	Don't call her that
mr stevenson	I'm sorry, Mick, Linda's crying, comfort her
linda	I'm not
mr stevenson	She's been crying. You look after her, look after the women here, and all the babies and try to give up smoking, I'm going off now to have some fun, leave all the little ladies behind
	Why did she always let the loonies inside her house?
mickey	I don't know
mr stevenson	Yes, I'm sorry Mick, nothing personal, you wouldn't like that lot from the day centre in your house either would you?
	MICKEY MOVES OFF
mr stevenson	(CALLS AFTER HIM) And your old Mum and Dad
mickey	What about them?
mr stevenson	Let them die in peace, pile coats on top of them when it gets cold, that's all they ask
linda	Mickey I love you!... What about all the abortions I've had
mickey	What about them?
linda	Don't you think that ought to make you feel a bit of responsibility?
mickey	It's a free country
mr stevenson	Mick, tell her you love her, you'll do anything for her, win her back
mickey	(GOES)
mr stevenson	Has he gone?
linda	Yes
mr stevenson	Forever do you think? (smiles)

★   ★   ★

END OF PART ONE

PART TWO

mickey	(STAGGERS FORWARD)
	I have returned (SITS ON THE FLOOR, STANDS)
	Friends? (LAUGHS) They're here somewhere...
	Where I don't know... (LOOKS ABOUT BLINDLY)
	This life...
	Right this is it, I'm going to bust this thing now (CALLS) I'm home!... Oh forget it (TURNS, FAINTS, UNCONSCIOUS)

LINDA COMES IN WHEELING AN EMPTY PUSHCHAIR

SOUNDS OF CHILDREN AGED 2 OR 3, SOUND STOPS

SHE CALLS HER CHILDREN AFTER HER

linda	(LAZILY) Come on
	(KIND AND COAXING) Come on

SHE ROLLS A CIGARETTE, HOLDS IT SMILES AHEAD OF HER

MICKEY STANDS

mickey	I have returned

HE WALKS AWAY STIFFLY, BLINDLY, LISTING TO THE LEFT HIS HAND UP TO HIS EYES LIKE A VIZOR

linda	I'm over here
mickey	(STOPS) Don't look at me while I'm dreaming it spoils the effect
linda	Mickey, Mickey I'm here
mickey	Give us a break please; there's a bloke down the road...
linda	What bloke?
mickey	In fact there's a load of blokes down the road. (LAUGHS)
linda	Come on darlings, come to mummy (SHE TURNS ABOUT HER, NO CHILDREN)
mickey	It is the mother.. a world of things picking at the children... defenceless
linda	Hurry up loves
mickey	Where's..

120

linda	Mickey
mickey	.. Peter Piper?
linda	Let's go inside..
mickey	No
	Where's the girl?
linda	Listen Mickey, Please..
mickey	I came back
linda	Mickey come here, come here, I want to whisper you something
mickey	No
linda	Come on... I'm going to a party
mickey	Look, whoever you are -
linda	Want to..? (GESTURES RUDELY)
mickey	(MOVES BLINDLY TO THE PUSHCHAIR)
linda	(STOPS HIM) Mickey, Mickey, tell you what.. I'm not wearing a bra
mickey	Got no tits
linda	Like a boy
mickey	Would you crawl in the other direction, I'm attending to my children.. Hello babies...
linda	You've been gone, I've got myself a bald man with a motorbike. He gives it to me from -
mickey	So what? So have I, he lets me kick it when I'm blue (MOVES NEARER TO THE PUSHCHAIR. LISTENS) What was that?
linda	(LISTENS)
mickey	A fart from far off. (WHILE SHE IS DISTRACTED BY THIS REMARK HE STUMBLES THE REMAINING STEPS TO THE PUSHCHAIR AND BOOTS IT SO IT FLIES ACROSS THE GROUND)
linda	(SHE MAKES TO STOP HIM BUT IT'S TOO LATE)
mickey	(SMILES AT HER) A dog barks, the wind blows it away....... What about this party then? Are we abnormal or something, no-one invites us

linda	You haven't been around
mickey	Don't tell me you've got friends, I'm your only fucking friend. Where are the children?
linda	They are stars in the sky
mickey	Very funny. (LAUGHS)
linda	I wrote you a poem
mickey	I thought I could smell piss in your knickers
linda	That's because I love you
mickey	(HOLDS ONE HAND TO HIS EAR AS IF HE'S HOLDING EARPHONES, WITH THE OTHER HE MAKES A VIZOR FOR HIS BLIND EYES, HE SINKS WITHIN HIMSELF)
linda	Warm isn't it, for evening. And we're all dusty and dirty. I took the kiddies for a walk to the playground, feed the ducks: stupid ducks, they ate a whole wonderloaf and started sinking
mickey	(STILL LISTENING TO THE IMAGINARY MUSIC IN HIS IMAGINARY HEADPHONES)
linda	Then one of the other kids in the park picked up a johnny and put it in his mouth
mickey	(STILL HEADPHONES, HE WHISPERS SOFTLY, THEN LOUDER) Crash, crash, crash, crash!
linda	His mum went spare
mickey	Kaboom! (NODS) Listen, listen
	(THE ENGINE OF A LARGE MOTORBIKE FAR OFF)
linda	What's that?
mickey	Me arriving. Broom, Broom! (HE PLAYS AT RIDING A MOTORCYCLE, A BROAD GRIMACE ON HIS FACE. HE SUDDENLY WEAKENS, A COLD NAUSEA DESTROYS HIM, HE FADES TO NOTHING, THEN RETURNS WITH BORROWED STRENGTH) How's your daddy?
linda	He's -
mickey	I hope you don't let your old daddy kiss your bum when you walk past his dying bed
linda	I smooth his pillow for him

mickey	I'll smooth his pillow for him
linda	(SLINKS UP TO HIM) Mickey..
mickey	You may as well keep it, I'm only here to celebrate..
linda	Yeah? What is there to celebrate?
mickey	In 1953 a little thing happened.. I was born
linda	1953? You're too young
mickey	That's the modern world, you're too young, too old, too black too white.. too fucking lazy.. get me a bottle
linda	Can't you do it in a corner?
mickey	A corner? I couldn't find a corner
linda	I'll show you
mickey	Let me in..
linda	No, Mickey
mickey	Why not? Don't you think I came all this way to see you? I've even got you a present. Look, look here, (SEARCHES HIS POCKETS) here's some.. What do you want?... I couldn't keep away to tell you the truth, wondering where you were, what you were doing
linda	I see
mickey	Tell you the truth your well known hospitality was eating up my bollocks. Point me to the door
linda	(POINTS AWAY) There
mickey	Liar. (WALKS BLINDLY IN THE OPPOSITE DIRECTION TOWARDS THE HOUSE)
linda	Mickey I want to make this as painless as possible
mickey	Yeah?
linda	So I won't let you come in
mickey	Look, there's your daddy reading the headlines
linda	You can't see him he's on a mattress
mickey	Always on a mattress your dad, bed sores, worms in his ears the whole lot
linda	Yeah and so have I, even the kiddies, so, we've got enough trouble. All you care about is the state of my private parts

mickey	There's nothing private there my dear..... You don't understand the love of the mature man, it's... getting to know them and watching them suffer it's a deep love of all human kind
linda	You don't love <u>me</u> then?
mickey	I love.. Your sad, dull, painful life my dear
linda	It sounds really good Mickey
mickey	Look, let's get it moving: How are you? Nice? What've you been doing? I hope you haven't had too much leisure time
linda	Why not?
mickey	I know what you do with it, on your back, legs in the air... is that why your thing always smells like a bath mat? Is it? Let me stay..
linda	I've really got to go now, nice of you to call round
mickey	Come on Linda (HE PUTS HIS HAND AROUND HER THIGH AND SQUEEZES UNTIL IT HURTS HER)
linda	Ow!
mickey	(STILL GRIPPING) Don't walk off. Go on feel that. We go to the pictures, no money, no money, but I'm happy, we are happy, we love each other, we are brothers, sisters
linda	(BITES HER LIP IN PAIN)
mickey	(LETS GO) Ah Linda, I cannot match your love... But I'll be a cousin to you, you can wash my shoes in the tumble drier, and I'll do you a few favours in return - fair? ok
	(HE FALLS TO THE GROUND)
linda	Christ Mickey (HOBBLES A FEW STEPS AWAY, LIMPING FROM A DEADENED THIGH) What's the matter?

SILENCE

Mickey?

SOUND OF A MOTORBIKE CRASHING NEARBY

LINDA LIMPS TO WHERE THE PUSHCHAIR IS AND PICKS IT UP

MICKEY ROLLS ONTO HIS BACK

I'm sorry Mickey, it's party time for me, all my friends.. They are waiting for me. I'll change when I get there... In fact I won't bother... I like a drink though, cor yeah.. Come back any time, kiddies love a daddy. I nearly forgot my poem, here it is:

> Mickey
>
> Got Sticky
>
> In his little Dicky
>
> Who put the scratch
>
> In my snatch

Why Don't you clap?

mickey	I've only got the one working arm

LINDA WALKS OFF CALLING HER CHILDREN

linda   Darlings, little loves

MICKEY SQUATS SHIVERING

MR STEVENSON COMES IN WITH A HEAVY STICK. HE SEES MICKEY AND APPROACHES FROM BEHIND SHAKING AND SHUDDERING WITH EFFORT AND RAGE. HE RAISES HIS STICK TO STRIKE AT MICKEY'S HEAD

mickey   (LOOKING UP) Oh. Who are you waving to?

mr stevenson (LOWERS HIS STICK WALKS AWAY)

mickey   (GETTING TO HIS FEET) I was just saying to your daughter.....

mr stevenson Go away..

mickey   I have returned

mr stevenson Welcome

mickey   (HIS HAND LIKE A VIZOR THE OTHER OUTSTRETCHED TO FEEL)

mr stevenson I must return to my mattress

mickey   I was just saying to your daughter -

mr stevenson Do you mind, we're expecting visitors

mickey   Let's be friends shall we?

mr stevenson No, please try to understand

ENTER LINDA DRESSED FOR A PARTY POSSIBLY

linda   What do you think Mickey?

mickey	(TO MR STEVENSON) Where's..?
mr stevenson	She's not well
linda	Mickey, my dress..
mickey	(INDICATES LINDA) Poor cow eh?
mr stevenson	(LOOKS AT MICKEY)
linda	Mickey, my dress...
mickey	I can't bloody see it can I?
linda	Let's go
mickey	(TO MR STEVENSON) You think I gave her a hard time?
mr stevenson	Linda, I'm going inside, close all the doors, bolt the windows
linda	I'm sick of it
mr stevenson	One last time, please here take my elbow
linda	Mickey, take a taxi, in a few moments we'll be free, no-one will find us
mickey	I don't know of a rank, my arms won't lift and I can't whistle
linda	Here take my hand
	DOES SO
linda	There. Doesn't that make you feel as if you could do anything you liked?
mickey	Did I tell you there's something wrong with your daughter?
mr stevenson	Linda I shall die if you don't help me
mickey	I'm off
mr stevenson	At least guide me to the door... I made you unhappy, and who has made me unhappy?
linda	I know a party we can go to
mickey	Sorry love, I left my tutu in the casualty ward
linda	We can have fun like we used to
mr stevenson	Welcome home my boy, welcome home
mickey	Well I'm not staying
mr stevenson	Come inside...

mickey	Stop staring at me Linda
linda	I can't help it
mr stevenson	...and leave the wicked world outside, a child of mine needn't concern herself with the world at large. Cruel beasts wander and..... a child of mine... you understand Mick

A DOOR SLAMS

Doors slam rudely in the wind. What did I achieve? I count my friends on one hand..

mickey	(WALKS OFF BLINDLY)
mr stevenson	(SEIZES MICKEY BY THE ARM AND WON'T LET GO) And there'll only be one car in my funeral procession.. Mick, wait for me I'll come with you
linda	Mickey wait
mickey	I'm not going anywhere!
mr stevenson	Take care of your things Linda, remember to switch off the oven, have you harmed the baby today, something you said? You should be careful. Have you ever thought, the damage we do to our children
linda	Take me away from it Mickey I can't stand it any more
mickey	Well Mr Stevenson How about a cup of tea?
mr stevenson	Certainly my boy, certainly

THEY WALK TOWARDS THE HOUSE TOGETHER

You want to come in for it I expect.. yes, yes.. You've been gone a long time, why come back at all.. you don't mind me asking?

THEY DISAPPEAR INSIDE

linda	Stop, get out of my house, get out!

JENINE APPROACHES

jenine	(SHE PUTS HER ARM AROUND LINDA) You look so small, it doesn't matter what they do, you're right not to let them in
linda	Jenine
jenine	Do you want me to help you? I've got nothing to do this morning. Shall I baby-sit or something. Look I brought this (GETS OUT A

CHILD'S PULLOVER FROM A PLASTIC BAG) yesterday for....

linda   Where did you get it?

jenine   I bought it

linda   Did you? You found it?

jenine   No, I bought it

linda   Where did you find it?

jenine   I didn't find it

linda   It's been used

jenine   I got it in a shop

linda   Why don't you say you found it?

jenine   I bought it. I don't care

linda   I do

jenine   Why? It doesn't matter

linda   You found it

jenine   Somewhere

linda   Why not just say?

jenine   I did. It doesn't matter

linda   Thanks anyway, it's nice, nice colours, bit warm for the summer

jenine   Linda, lend me five pounds, I've got to have five pounds I've got no
           cigs

linda   (PUTS HAT ON) You spend all your time begging cigarettes

jenine   Yes, it's so degrading, you know I'm really educated, they think
           I'm a tart but really.... keep the cigs. Please help me. You do trust
           me don't you? Why are you sad today?....

linda   I have to be alone Jenine

jenine   I have to be alone, I have to get away, they want to give me electric
           shocks. That won't cure me because there's nothing wrong with
           me, I just need a lot of money and good living, I was born to it, I was
           adopted by the wrong people, I needed people with class, anyway
           give me £5 and I'll tidy up here for you, you look so lonely, I know

how it feels. I've been lonely. You go and sleep and I'll take care of everything. You used to be pretty and so did I but when life gets difficult you lose your looks. Feel my hands, they're shaking, it's all the ice they put down my back, it hurts so much, but they say it's to take away the pain. What pain? I ask them (LINDA WALKS AWAY, JENINE GRABS HER) I hear a dog barking in the street and it's the same old story, I know who it is, it's the wolves, they've got her by the scruff of the neck, they took her away, they got jealous, outraged as these people so often are. I can hear them shouting out there, calling my name but I'm not going to go out to them, I can say I thought it was voices in my head. They think I really do hear voices but that's just the way the wind tunes in like with a radio. I had a radio down by the rushes by the bridge, a stick like a divining rod, they'd given her to some jews and they'd just left her, I had to look after her all by myself. There's something not quite right there isn't there? They put you into care and then they try to make you work for them. I said listen, if I want to I can take her to my mother so don't stand over me checking if I know what I'm doing because I do know, I know and I've done it all before. They thought she was my first because I look so young, they always said what a beautiful complexion I had... I let them take her in the end, well I just couldn't be bothered, they wanted me to carry the shit around in a bag, I'm not doing that I said, how would you like the smell all the time? It's lovely, it's like sour milk they said. How would they bloody know? They're all as dry as parchment, no-one would be able to stick anything up there and get it down again so I know that for certain, If I get £5 now I'll go to Kensington, I need make up, have you got any? No, you don't need it. No we all could do with it, why not? Come on, let's go out and buy some together. Why do you look so sad? Let me take care of you. Do you know what Mickey said to me, he said you see that girl in there?, she's like a whirlwind in my heart, and when I look at her she's like a bottle opener in my eye

linda   Did you notice Mickey has come back?

jenine   Yes I noticed him by the door

linda	You didn't say anything about it
jenine	I'd rather be here with you
linda	Jenine, I'm sorry (THEY EMBRACE) Thanks for coming round
jenine	Shall I go?
linda	I don't know, stay
jenine	You can't think of anything else but him
linda	Who Jenine?
jenine	Mickey, Mickey's come back

MICKEY STAGGERS OUT BLINDLY ONTO THE STEP

★   ★   ★

NIGHT OUTSIDE THE HOUSE, THEN INSIDE

MICKEY ARRIVES OUTSIDE IN THE DARK, THE SHADOW OF AN OLD MAN GOES PAST, HE IS BEATING HIS DOG

mickey	Bloody old pooch, hit the bleeder

THE SHADOW STOPS BEATING HIS DOG, WALKS AWAY GETTING SMALLER AND SMALLER

Ah I can see!

LOOKS ABOUT HIM

No I can't. Where is everything? Shsh. Quiet, evening Constable, yes (SMILES) all the girls in their summer dresses I see. Oh yes? Got yourself a cosy little number then, you pop across the road for a quick one? Mmm she is a lovely girl yes, I know I was just saying how her well known hospitality was eating up my... ability to concentrate

No I can't see a thing

A LATE BIRD SINGS IN A TREE

Oh a bird singing in a tree

Where's he gone? (HE STAGGERS FORWARD BLINDLY AND IS INSIDE THE ROOM)

What's this? A sofa? Suddenly I'm indoors

Who's leg? What kind of a welcome do you call this? A leg out-stretched in the dark. I'm going now, clean up in here a bit will you.

I've heard all the streets, the way they behave, and St. Peters street, I can't be bothered shouting at them

Is it dark in here or what? Where's Linda, what've you been saying to her?

No-one understands me that's my trouble

I remember one time Linda and I were trying to get some peace and this geezer comes jumping through the window shooting his mouth off saying he's going to shoot me, I've got a room full of crossbows he says I'll go and fetch one, this blinking neighbourhood

A LARGE MOTORBIKE GOES PAST, IT'S HEADLIGHT SHINES INTO THE ROOM

(WATCHES THE LIGHT AS IT FILLS THE ROOM) Oh look, a sandy beach. (SEARCHES HIS POCKETS) Where is everything?

JENINE IS IN THE ROOM SITTING ON A CHAIR IN THE CORNER

Listen have you stolen my cigarettes?

jenine	(NO REPLY)
mickey	Oh. Have you got a cigarette or what?
	I mean I just ask you a question and you - would you run over to the garage and get some?
jenine	Don't hurt me
mickey	What are you trying to pull here? I'm ill actually, I'm going to have a lie down
jenine	(SAYS NOTHING)
mickey	What? Who? Yes she's here somewhere, have a look, I'm recently blind. Even my hearing is dodgy. Music in one ear my own voice in the other. You're in my way I'd like to stumble about in peace. Is who here?
jenine	(MUMBLES A NAME)
mickey	No but her mum will be here soon, our children too, her father, all

	her relations, we're planning a party, a family do, party games, old people the whole lot
jenine	(CRIES OUT SUDDENLY) Alright Mickey
	MICKEY SITS DOWN ON THE FLOOR
	JENINE WALKS OUT OF THE ROOM
mr stevenson	You look ill
mickey	I am. I am ill
	PAUSE
mr stevenson	Mickey, Mickey. please lend me your shoulder, I'm sorry if, just now I... but now I see in you myself when I was a young man...
mickey	(LAUGHS)
mr stevenson	I'm being friendly to you.... You can sleep here if you like, have the pick of anything that's going. You don't even have to help around the house
mickey	Thanks a lot
mr stevenson	(GRIPS HIS ARM) You'll wish you could have found it in your heart to... just a little sympathy you know... goes a long way
mickey	Where's Linda?
mr stevenson	Not here at least. Tell me.... You have two women...
mickey	I need a third..
mr stevenson	Can't help you there, this isn't a brothel
mickey	No
mr stevenson	No, this is my home
mickey	A doss house
mr stevenson	If you want to bring some furniture you are welcome. A few sticks would be more than welcome, yes. Come, sit on the bed..
mickey	Stop touching me
mr stevenson	I could help you make a lot of money, more than I have. I don't begrudge it you, a young man should be free and have a full heart and full pockets, you see?

mickey	I see
mr stevenson	Oo oo I have a pain here in my arm
mickey	Oh
mr stevenson	What do you think it is?
mickey	Heart attack
mr stevenson	Yes, yes!
mickey	It wouldn't be the first
mr stevenson	What are you talking about, I've had a life of them, don't talk to me my boy about heart attacks
mickey	Have you seen my children?
mr stevenson	Linda has them. They tire her out. Her face is worn, her tits are sagging. Have you come to save her perhaps?
mickey	Do me a favour!
mr stevenson	Don't stand there by the window looking out, you clutter my view
	MICKEY GOES TO THE DOOR
	What shall I tell her?
	Linda. Shall I tell her you're gone out? Will be back after the dark, in the morning. if Linda asks?
mickey	I don't care what you tell her
mr stevenson	Did she go out with friends?
mickey	Eh?
mr stevenson	That leaves you free for the other one
mickey	I know. That's why I've got her lined up
mr stevenson	Have you?
mickey	What?
mr stevenson	Got her fixed up
mickey	Yes, got her fixed up
mr stevenson	For tonight, just like that?
mickey	Yes. Want to come?
mr stevenson	Come? Me?

mickey	Yes
mr stevenson	What... Why yes, yes, I'd come. Where are we going?
mickey	Nowhere
mr stevenson	Nowhere?...... Oh but who'll open the door to Linda?
mickey	She has a key
mr stevenson	But who'll make up her bed?
mickey	What? She's got a bed?
mr stevenson	The kids then, who'll see to them?
mickey	Fuck the kids
mr stevenson	Alright then
mickey	Yeah, let her deal with that
mr stevenson	Who?
mickey	Linda
mr stevenson	Yeah, let Linda deal with it

*   *   *

MICKEY AND LINDA WALKING ARM IN ARM BY THE EDGE OF A LAKE

mickey	This must be the 500th time we've done this
linda	Yes
mickey	...It always ends up the same way though doesn't it?
linda	...
mickey	..Still never mind. You and me, lovers from prehistoric times until yesterday... no I mean forever and ever
	PAUSE
	What's the matter? Stomach ache?
linda	Yes
mickey	Earache?
linda	(SIGHS RUBS HER HAND ON HER STOMACH) I feel...
mickey	You feel...? What?
linda	I feel...

mickey	There's always something bloody wrong
linda	I can't help it
mickey	I know. (STROKES HER HEAD) Never mind, poor little baby, nothing's quite right is it?
linda	(PAINED EXPRESSION SEARCHING INSIDE FOR THE SEAT OF THE PAIN) I... just
mickey	Yes
linda	I feel...
mickey	Oh I know. Poor thing
linda	(LOOKS AT HIM, DROPS HER EYES TO THE GROUND TO HIDE HER ANGER)
mickey	So anyway I said to this geezer I can see you like living down the road from her, alright mate, you may think you're doing her a favour but you ain't 'cause she don't need no favours doing, she's all bloody favours all day long. Oh. Aren't you listening?
linda	Yes
mickey	Don't just let me ramble on on my own
linda	I...
mickey	(STOPS HER) I mean don't...
linda	I...
mickey	(STOPS HER) I mean what kind of a life is this...
linda	I...
mickey	(STOPS HER) Really? For me?
linda	Mickey I...
mickey	Look at that water, what a stinking hole
linda	(LOOKS WITHOUT SEEING, BLINDED BY HER THOUGHTS)
mickey	Don't just pretend to look. Rags everywhere, in the reeds, look rags, rag dolls, little things wrapped in rags, aren't you interested? Look there's a little rag doll in the water floating along, look at it, don't just, a real bloody... lying there, someone must have put it there, it didn't bloody arrive by itself
linda	Yes

mickey	Don't just say yes, look at it
linda	(LOOKS)
mickey	No, look because you want to see it. It's not every day you see a real rag doll
linda	Mmm
mickey	Go on pick it up, alright I'll pick it up. (PICKS IT UP, HANDS IT TO HER) There, there, look after it or something....
linda	(SHE HOLDS IT ABSENTLY)
mickey	(SNATCHES IT FROM HER) If you can't forget about yourself just for one moment, then I'll... No I won't, I don't care about bleeding rag dolls (THROWS IT IN THE WATER)

STARES AFTER IT

LINDA PRETENDS TO STARE AFTER IT TOO BUT SHE DOESN'T SEE IT BECAUSE SHE IS THINKING

I said I don't care about rag dolls

linda	(SHE STARES AT HIM PASSIVELY)
mickey	You bloody evil bitch
linda	(SHE STARES)
mickey	Aren't you happy out here? I thought we'd go for a walk together...
linda	Shall I go and change?
mickey	Do what you like
linda	Shall I put my hair in a pony tail?
mickey	Yes do that
linda	I'm sorry Mickey, It's when I feel you don't appreciate me

THEY ARRIVE AT WHERE JENINE IS CROUCHING BY THE SHALLOWS DIPPING SOMETHING INTO THE WATER

mickey	What are you doing?
jenine	I'm trying to wash my heart. (SHE GETS UP, HER PEACE DISTURBED, DROPS THE HEART INTO THE WATER) Why haven't you been to see me? You seem to be cooling off, that's never happened before. I suppose

you're tired of it all. I am. Linda is. You must be

PAUSE. SHE SMILES, THEN CHANGES

Oh Mickey, it's so painful, it's worse than ever, look what it's done to me.. I'm Linda's slave now aren't I Linda?

linda	She does me little favours
jenine	In exchange for cigarettes
linda	Yes we're friends again
jenine	She's the model for my phantom pregnancies, look. (SHE SMOOTHES HER CLOTHES OVER THE CURVE OF HER BELLY)
linda	How that little bulge used to scare me
jenine	Yes, now it's Linda that scares me
linda	- and that's the way it should be
jenine	Isn't it Mickey?
mickey	(NO REPLY)
jenine	Don't worry. I'm sure there's fun and games left in the future. You don't need to take this seriously it's not the end of anything. I'm sure we'll manage something no one else has ever managed
linda	Shall we invite Jenine to dinner Mickey?
jenine	I can come and eat the crumbs from your table
linda	Yes and we'll get to know each other all over again
jenine	I hope I can behave as well as I've behaved just now
linda	She's been alright hasn't she Mickey?
jenine	So has Mickey
linda	Mickey? Oh no, he's alright

MICKEY TURNS AND WALKS AWAY

jenine	(CALLS AFTER HIM) I'll try not to be a baby

SHE RETURNS TO THE WATERS EDGE

★　　★　　★

A TABLE SET. MR STEVENSON, JENINE AND MICKEY SIT ALREADY, LINDA COMES OUT DOWN THE STEPS

linda	There, the children are asleep in their little beds
mr stevenson	Good we can begin. (TUCKS NAPKIN) What are we celebrating?
linda	Mickey's come home
jenine	Mickey's birthday
mr stevenson	(TO LINDA) Come on come on. Here sit on my knee pet
mickey	Get your hands off her
jenine	Mickey
mickey	Yes my flaxen haired angel?
mr stevenson	How are we all feeling?
linda	Fine
jenine	..Please sit next to me
	PAUSE
mickey	..Of course
mr stevenson	Linda would you feed me..?
linda	Oh...
mr stevenson	Only the difficult bits..
mickey	I can hear the kids crying
mr stevenson	No you can't
mickey	Yes I can
mr stevenson	You're just making it up. You go if it's that important
mickey	I didn't say it's important, I said I can hear them. Shall <u>I</u> feed you?
mr stevenson	No I want her to do it, my daughter
mickey	Shall I feed you Jenine
jenine	No, I don't...
mr stevenson	Yes you feed her
linda	I think I heard them
mickey	Did you?
jenine	Where are <u>my</u> babies?
	PAUSE

mickey	If you heard them go and see
jenine	Mickey...
linda	Food anyone
mr stevenson	How lovely she serves. You look so well my dear. (LINDA SERVES MR STEVENSON) Thank you Linda, that's very nice
linda	Jenine?
jenine	No, I'm not hungry
mr stevenson	Linda's got lovely fat arms now...

LINDA SITS, THEY EAT, PAUSE

Linda you're not concentrating, your soup is running down your front

SHE CARRIES ON EATING

Linda!

jenine	I'll just have a banana
mickey	What are you eating a banana for?
jenine	Why not?
mr stevenson	Linda, by the way where's the -
mickey	Wine
mr stevenson	The wine, yes where's the wine?
linda	There's none left, I drank it
mr stevenson	You drank it?
jenine	Get me some
linda	There isn't any Jenine
jenine	It is your babies crying I can hear
mickey	Yes I can too
linda	Let them cry
mr stevenson	Poor little darlings, need a cry I should think
linda	Bleeders
jenine	I just want to have a -

linda	A what?
jenine	A look
linda	Go on then
jenine	Is there any wine?
mickey	She's drunk it all
linda	Yes and now I feel sleepy
jenine	I'll take a look then. (DOESN'T MOVE)
mr stevenson	Linda, you're not feeding me
linda	I need a sleep, a few minutes should do it

LINDA CLIMBS ONTO THE TABLE AND LIES DOWN

mr stevenson	How can you display yourself like this
mickey	(KEEPS ON EATING)
mr stevenson	Didn't I bring you up to be shy?
linda	(FALLING ASLEEP) Yes...
mr stevenson	Your dress has ridden up over your thighs. (HE CATCHES SIGHT OF MICKEY) Mickey! You have had more than your fair share of strawberries
mickey	Have I?
mr stevenson	Yes
mickey	I took exactly the same as Linda. I knew you'd be watching me
mr stevenson	Linda can take as many as she likes
jenine	Mickey I brought you a potted plant
mickey	Thank you
jenine	It's a geranium. Put it in the window to show that love's poison never dies
mr stevenson	Didn't you use to carry around a neat little black handbag?
jenine	I dropped it...
mr stevenson	..and go everywhere in a taxi?
jenine	Yes
mr stevenson	And now you are cadging cigarettes I hear

140

jenine	So many wolves around my breaking heart... Still at least <u>you</u> are happy Mickey. I remember when you would pretend to be blind, you were so coarse and rude, now all your aggression has faded, isn't that nice?
mickey	(STANDS) Would you like to walk along the beach with me?
jenine	I'm married now
mickey	Are you? (SITS)
jenine	You don't mind?
mickey	Children?
jenine	There's one in my womb at this very moment
mickey	Ah
jenine	The size of a pea...
mickey	It's not mine? Is it?
jenine	It couldn't be
mickey	Of course not
	PAUSE
mickey	Are you sure you have a child inside you the size of a pea?
jenine	Not one hundred percent
mickey	There is some uncertainty?
mr stevenson	Stop this at once!
jenine	Be quiet Mr Stevenson, You'll wake Linda
mr stevenson	She ought to be awake... and cover herself up
jenine	She's happy the way she is
mr stevenson	She's such a whore
mickey	Rubbish
jenine	It makes her feel happy and free Mr Stevenson to have something people want. It's an expression of... her inner light...
mr stevenson	Come, come
jenine	Of the soul that burns behind her shifty eyes, the dullest, most lifeless eyes...
mr stevenson	(HAS STOPPED LISTENING, SHAKES LINDA TO WAKE HER) Linda, Linda!

jenine	...apart from your own.. and if you set her free she'll burst into flames like a -
mickey	(STROKING LINDA'S HEAD) ...Piece of toast
jenine	...and live... and love
mr stevenson	I don't wish to hear
jenine	..with an open heart
mr stevenson	It's obscene. Don't you think I know my own daughter
jenine	Linda's tired because she is pregnant
mickey	Yes
mr stevenson	Ah no, sadly the little pink patches in her knickers tell us otherwise, yes. (STROKES LINDA'S HEAD)
jenine	No baby? But there has to be! I've taught myself to love it, it has cost me so much!
mr stevenson	Oh, there is a little baby the size of a pea, but it's not as big as it should be.. and the little love has pains too... I feel them as well of course...
jenine	There is a baby..
mr stevenson	But it's dead, dead but clinging on nevertheless
jenine	No! please!
mr stevenson	We've arranged to have it scraped out haven't we lovey?
mickey	Can I be there. I am the father. I hope
mr stevenson	It's not a spectator sport my boy... They use a kind of hoover I believe...
mickey	Oh well...
jenine	(CRIES) But I wanted her to have this baby
	PAUSE, JENINE SOBS BITTERLY
mr stevenson	Well who's going to do the washing up?
mickey	Linda............ Lazy tart
mr stevenson	Why are you crying? is it sympathy for my daughter?
jenine	(CRYING) No, no.... Yes

mr stevenson It's not the end of the world. They'll have many more

MICKEY EATS THE LEFTOVERS AND DRAINS THE LAST GLASS OF SQUASH

jenine Yes

mr stevenson I'll buy them a car one day, I think, make them like a real family, you know

jenine Yes

mr stevenson ....Linda has started dressing smartly, have you noticed?

jenine Yes I have noticed

mr stevenson (HE RUNS HIS HAND ALONG THE SLEEPING LINDA) See her skirt, and these shoes? She's a lovely girl isn't she?

jenine (DRIES HER EYES, STANDS UP, GATHERS HERSELF) Actually, I'm tired of hearing that. I think she's plain

mr stevenson Her very plainness seems to attract. Look at Mickey... He's like a dog chasing after a b -

jenine No... She's very average

mr stevenson ...chasing after a bitch on heat... You must have noticed

jenine I don't think about it...

mr stevenson Sit down. Aren't you well?

JENINE SITS DOWN. MICKEY DRINKS A FLAGON OF WATER. MR STEVENSON LOOKS AT HIM WITH IRRITATION

jenine I think..

mr stevenson You think?

jenine I think.. Mickey is wasted on her. He's fooling himself if he thinks-

mr stevenson If he thinks..?

jenine ...he'll get anything out of her

MR STEVENSON THINKS. PAUSE

mr stevenson Get what out of her?

MICKEY CONSUMES SOME GRAPES

jenine I think he feels invisible

mr stevenson (TO MICKEY) Could you pass me a grape

mickey	None left
jenine	Do you know what I mean?
mr stevenson	What? (HE HAS FORGOTTEN SHE IS THERE)
jenine	About Mickey, you see I don't think he's very happy, in fact he can never be -
mr stevenson	(TO MICKEY) What?
jenine	Not with her
mr stevenson	Not one?
mickey	No
mr stevenson	Sponger
jenine	I admit, I'm not any better for him myself now
mr stevenson	I'll throw you out of this house one day
jenine	...But that's because I'm paralysed by the pain of my broken heart
mr stevenson	You have devoured my fruit my boy
jenine	But if got the chance I'd be perfect
mr stevenson	You've spoiled my garden with your motorcycle

MICKEY BITES INTO AN APPLE

LINDA SNORES

You've ploughed furrows in my lawn

jenine	I'd be perfect! (STANDS UP AND SWEEPS THE CROCKERY OFF THE TABLE)

SHORT PAUSE. MR STEVENSON LOOKS AT HER

(MORE CALMLY) Mickey is frightened to change anything for the better, you see

mr stevenson	I think I'll awaken Linda. (HE SLIDES HIS HAND ACROSS THE TABLE TO HER FOOT. MICKEY SNATCHES UP MR STEVENSON'S WALKING STICK AND BRINGS IT DOWN WITH A CRACK UPON MR STEVENSON'S HAND)

Oh my hand, my hand, he's broken my hand

BLOOD STREAMS FROM HIS HAND

Look all my fingers are twisted. You madman

MICKEY STANDS BEFORE JENINE. SHE STROKES HIS CHEEK

jenine	Is that the best you can do?
mr stevenson	How dare you intrude upon my person. (HE STANDS UP) My stick is snapped in half, how will I walk?

HE STAGGERS FROM THE TABLE

HE STAGGERS BACK AGAIN

I shall wake her, I shall wake her, Linda, wake up darling, look at what has happened

LINDA WAKES UP WITH A START, HER FACE CONTORTED MOMENTARILY BY IMBECILITY WHICH PASSES AS SHE BECOMES FULLY AWAKE TWO SECONDS LATER

linda	What?
mr stevenson	Look at Daddy's hand
linda	Oh what's happened?
mr stevenson	Come and help me inside my dear, I'm in shock

LINDA SITS UP ON THE TABLE. MR STEVENSON HELPS HER AS SHE SLIDES SLEEPILY TO THE GROUND, HE CATCHES HER IN HIS ARMS AND PULLS DOWN THE DRESS WHICH HAS RUMPLED UP IN THE PROCESS

mr stevenson	We'll go and have a little sleep on the mattress

LINDA CATCHES SIGHT OF MICKEY AND JENINE STANDING FIVE FEET APART STARING INTO EACH OTHERS EYES

linda	Wait, what are they doing?
jenine	It's alright Linda I was just saying goodbye
mr stevenson	Do help me Linda, I'm bleeding, look
linda	You're always saying goodbye
mr stevenson	(HOBBLES UP TO MICKEY) You're always saying goodbye. (HE WAVES HIS BLOODY HAND IN HIS FACE)
linda	I can't ever get any peace
mr stevenson	(TO MICKEY) Let me have some peace

PAUSE

Come on my baby, daddy's depressed, his knuckles are in shatters, we'll bathe them

LINDA TURNS TO GO WITH HIM CASTING A GLANCE OF HATRED AT HIM AS SHE DOES SO, WHICH PASSES WITHOUT HER NOTICING

THEY GO INSIDE TOGETHER

MICKEY STANDS WHERE HE IS WITHOUT MOVING, JENINE HAS THE AIR OF ONE ABOUT TO LEAVE

jenine   Mickey, that's Linda's old jumper isn't it?

mickey   Yes

jenine   (WITH TEARS AND ANGER) Take it off

MICKEY PULLS OFF THE JUMPER HE IS WEARING AND THEN JENINE WALKS AWAY

MICKEY SITS AT THE TABLE AND SEARCHES IDLY FOR MORE LEFT OVERS

THE END

First performed at Theatre de l'Odeon, Paris, in April 1995

cat and mouse (sheep)

A SMALL GREENGROCERS. A SEVENTY YEAR OLD WOMAN COMES INTO THE SHOP

old woman	Three pounds of aubergines please
gengis	Ah a dinner party I suppose?
old woman	That's right, a few meat-eating friends are coming round so we're having a big chicken salad
gengis	Sounds super
old woman	Can I have a bottle of cherryade on tick?
gengis	Certainly. Are you a bit short?
old woman	Yes my boyfriend has been made redundant again. That's the fifth time this year
gengis	Do you want these? They're alright but they've gone a funny colour. I usually make a stew with them
old woman	Mmm thanks. How m-
gengis	No have them
old woman	Oh thanks

SHE PAYS FOR THE AUBERGINES AND THEN GOES

gengis	I'm going to sell chickens in future
uncle	But next-door sells chickens
gengis	I can sell them cheaper
uncle	He'll be annoyed
gengis	He shouldn't charge so much, people round here can't afford it
uncle	He's greedy
gengis	He had that new floor put in for no reason, now he's got that loan to pay back
uncle	He's got to walk on something I suppose
gengis	What was he walking on before?
uncle	That's a good point
gengis	It's all his own fault
uncle	So, the gentleman's agreement is going to come to an end is it?

gengis	I've got to make a living too
uncle	You'll be stocking milk next
gengis	I will, and cheaper too
uncle	He'll be very put out
gengis	I can't help that anymore
uncle	It'll be war on this parade
gengis	And another thing
uncle	What's that nephew?
gengis	I'm moving out of that flat of his upstairs
uncle	Yes well it could be embarrassing, what with this price war and all
gengis	I'm sick of paying the rent
uncle	But where will you and Indira and the little horror live?
gengis	We'll live in the back room here
uncle	But it's only tiny. All of you in one small room. How cramped it will be!
gengis	We'll get by
uncle	But there's no window
gengis	We're rarely in, we're always here working
uncle	But there's no running water
gengis	There's a tap in the yard
uncle	There's no toilet
gengis	We'll go in a bucket and I'll carry it out to the nearest convenience
uncle	What does Indira say?
gengis	She's very excited
uncle	Darrin
gengis	Yes uncle?
uncle	Where will your aunty and I stay?
gengis	You can sleep in there with us
uncle	What kind of bed is it?

150

gengis	A large single
uncle	So that's you, Indira, Aunty, the baby and me all in one single?
gengis	A large single. I get up early anyway so you can all stretch out
uncle	Hardly stretch
gengis	Come and have a look
uncle	You've got the bed in already?
gengis	Yes, you'll be surprised how roomy it is
uncle	Alright

THEY GO AND LOOK IN THE BACK ROOM

PAUSE

THEY RETURN

uncle	Yes you're right. It's quite spacious after all

★　　★　　★

uncle	Well, how's it going with the old price war?
gengis	Things have changed a lot uncle
uncle	I see he's started stocking vegetables
gengis	I don't mind that. He still can't do 'em cheaper than me. And the quality of mine is better. I don't sell rubbish you know
uncle	He sells those bags of potatoes
gengis	They're rubbish they are. I've got all cold drinks in and jars of pickle and all the Indian stuff. It goes like a bomb
uncle	You've changed too. You're ambitious, a man building an empire. Do you think you're still the considerate chap you used to be?
gengis	I'm giving people good food cheap. I never rip anybody off
uncle	But what if he goes out of business? Then they won't have a grocer around here, they'll lose out. You'll never be able to stock everything he does. Everyone will have to walk miles to Sainsbury's
gengis	He won't go out of business, not if he watches himself
uncle	Life is harder now. I don't sleep
gengis	But we've got more money

uncle But I don't enjoy spending it anymore. I feel sorrow. Your aunty, she's always been a swinger, she loves the high life but I'm more your man with a book beside the fire, a bit of an intellectual, studious, high-minded moral type, a rear guard man, a thinker, a political animal, a fabian, a fundamentalist, I'm a justice fanatic a fan, I wear the right clothes, I'm left wing, I'm anti-semitic I'm anti this I'm anti that I'm a star fucker and I'm not above a bit of racism because I'm a campaigner and no-one will ever know not even myself you know what I mean because I'm interested in crystal balls and pot-pourri and Che Guevara and Mussolini and Winnie Mandela and co-operatives and things you stick on the fridge and notes and notelets and note pads and living in London because there's a really thriving bi-sexual community there and lots going on and I own my own home and I run a little car because I care and I could really fuck you up if you get in my way brother sister mother black white racist sexist bloody bastards the whole lot of them, call me Ms don't fuck with my possessions ok because they're all approved and everything's kosher and I'm on the right side of the fence and I don't read much but I like a good book about suffering Chinese or suffering anybody anyplace because you know what I mean, there's so much suffering isn't there and I earn a bit of extra cash working for this charity organization that recycles shit and sends the best of it to the niggers and magically makes a massive profit and that's ok because they're helping people and I believe in that so I'm doing my bit and earning a fast buck at the same time, that's the future you know, recycled rags for the little babies with flies on their eyes. We're all going to be so fucking rich and so fucking pleased with ourselves my pussy is going to explode with pure satisfaction and that's all you can do isn't it because the world is going to rack and ruin. It's criminal, it's a crime, all middle aged men ought to be in prison because people have to be free, you know what I mean, they have to think for themselves, I always do. All I want is enough money to do exactly what I want because the state owes me a living course they course they do course they fucking do. I pay my taxes, I'd willingly pay more, I was a bit of a punk rocker in my day, I went to all the gigs and I stapled my thumb, anyway they're all arms dealers and so would I be because deep inside I'm a poetical sort of a person, I'm a lyrical sort of a person, I'm a sensitive sort of a person, I'm a creative sort of a person and I know how to get some if you want some, but I've lost all interest in sex and I'm proud because I'm not going to be exploited and if I had any kids I'd put bromide in their tea because its all about degradation and men bore me and so I just say "look" you know what I mean and he said "look baby, its all just words, you're so afraid" and I said "typical man, look at the way you're dominating this argument" and then like the poof he was he went and cut his own throat with a Financial Times letter knife. I hate weak men. So don't come to me, because I look after number one ok?ok?ok?ok?ok? So don't blubber just because you want to be mothered because its not on offer so watch out because this is the cultural revolution and what's up is going to be down and what's down is going to be down even further, but all in name only because do you know what? Betting is immoral and those weaselly little Irishmen in the betting shops should be taken out and put to work digging holes in the road and made to do aikido. I'm doing a class in social awareness, Fuck you, you racist!

gengis	So uncle, what you are saying is you want a bed of your own
uncle	Yes
gengis	Alright I'll see what I can do

★   ★   ★

uncle	Your silken purse my darling is voluptuous to my fundament
aunty	Our nephew. He's like a tub of cream cheese
uncle	He's beautiful
aunty	Life is beautiful Ned
uncle	You're not uncomfortable with the new activities?
aunty	He's getting very frenzied in his movements, do you think he's gone mad
uncle	He's a man of the people if they did but know it

aunty	I hate people, they're so unfair and horrible. Give me animals any day. A little doggie for example, all hair-cut and shampooed doing its little shitty in my hand, aaah the poor love!
uncle	Shsh here's Gengis
aunty	Gengis darling, you look so low
gengis	Indira has left me
aunty	Oh no! Did she take the kid as well?
gengis	Yes
aunty	Thank God. I hate their shitty little bottoms. Are you a broken man now?
gengis	She said I'd made a big mistake, that she still loved me, that she'd never come back, that she hates a loser, hates a schmuck, hates a money grubber, hates me hates herself hates the baby hates the flat hates the single bed hates shops hates life
uncle	You've upset her haven't you
gengis	There's no going back now. I've nothing else to live for. I must put up new shelving
aunty	Darling
gengis	Yes?
aunty	Have you forgotten the charm of a quiet life?
gengis	Yes, completely. All I want now is destruction and victory and failure and death and victory and suffering and defeat and death and victory
aunty	Are we going to stay open later in the evenings?
gengis	We'll never close we'll never open. This will be 100% total shop, neither shop nor no shop
uncle	There's greatness in those words, Aunty
aunty	There's greatness in the lips that speak them
uncle	Greatness in the tongue and eyes that invent the words and send them to the teeth that cut them. The temples of his mind, the soles of his feet. He's ours now Aunty, our own boy

154

gengis   I am king

uncle   You are the Royal Emperor

gengis   I am khan

uncle   You are a cunt

gengis   I will die a cunt. I will die, the world will laugh. Blood will gurgle in that breath and she shall expire with me

★   ★   ★

IN THE PALACE OF THE MIGHTY KHAN

gengis   Uncle take me away from all this. I want to laugh and sing, I want I want to pull the legs off flies and burn them with a magnifying glass like the other children

uncle   Here take my hand Barry. I want to tell you something. Look around you son, what do you see?

gengis   Not much actually

uncle   That's right my boy because do you know? There isn't much left. There used to be things, but as you know its all been either broken or sold or sent somewhere else. There were things here boy that scum like you wouldn't recognize if it slapped you in the face. You hear what I'm telling you boy, you hear what I'm sayin'?

gengis   Yes I do sir

uncle   When I was your age this wasn't just paradise on earth this was the peak of fuckin' human achievement. We didn't just have busses, no sir we didn't just have flower fuckin' beds, though you bet your sweet life we had 'em, yes sir we had 'em. No we had something else. Shall I tell you what that something else was nephew child?

gengis   Tell it Sir

uncle   We had philosophy! Yes! We had art. Yes! We had politics and history and sociology; we had MUSIC. I can hear it now callin' to me over th' airwaves. There was music in the streets and parks, there was music in the stores and booteeks, at the railroad stops and the city squares and in the gleaming white hospitals full of ailin' folk a' convalessin' you know what we had there? You guessed it boy -Ding dong, pling plong bing bong dow de dow dow. We had white arsed muthafuckrs singin' the blues and blue nosed nigra fellas singin' their selves purple, we had chinkies that were kinky with their rinky tink tinky and Puerto Ricans and Mohecans makin' sounds that were out of bounds. And if ya didn't like it you know what ya did boy?

gengis   No sir

uncle   Ya went and ya fucked yourself, yes sir that's what yer did 'cause there wasn't no way no place you could git away from it because The People Were Telling It Like It Was you know what I'm sayin'?

gengis   I reckon I do unk

uncle   Now listen me boy and listen me good. I ain't gonna continny this here con-ver-sation. I ain't gonna go on an' itemise all of them things we had back there in th' good old golden days cuz I might embarrass you. I ain't gona say like as we had them librarees where folks come and pessued theys lernin and a-readin and a-lookin up thungs because there ain't no muthafuckr kin read no more in this nation

gengis   Get to the point uncle darling

uncle   The point is that what little remains of the great civilization that once held sway here I want you to think of as yours to dispose of how you will

gengis   I shall do

uncle   Good

gengis   What's that great blue thing outside the window uncle?

uncle   The sky

gengis   Remarkable how its changed. You see how it now seems to have a head and out of the top of its head, why look, it's raining!

uncle   Is it? No, that's a whale

gengis   Is it true they are why you can't get a council transfer even on medical grounds? Because they've given all the flats to the whales?

uncle   Yes it is true

gengis	What rotten luck for the plankton
uncle	Listen carefully boy; The plankton are scum. Evil and lascivious. They know nothing, feel less. My plan is to infect the gorgeous belly of the spermy leviathan with their odious little bodies until they are all beached, the mucousy little white scum and the great blue monster of carnal desire together. Then we shall haul them to the knackers' yard and make them into glue for my model aeroplanes
gengis	But aunty told me the whales cry most beautifully. Real tears. She has tapes
uncle	All fakes. Merely an ingenious amplification of her bowel movements set to music
gengis	She's a woman of many pretentions my aunt. Shall I have her liquidated?
uncle	Not yet boy, she may want to buy something. Now before I forget I want you to strip to your underwear
gengis	But uncle darling I told you I need time, sweet words, the odd bunch of flowers. I want to feel needed first
uncle	Gentle boy, be at ease, this is a purely altruistic deed on both our parts. You see, this fax came in
gengis	What is it? It's so beautiful!
uncle	It's a photo of an earthquake in Turkeytown, 10,000 dead
gengis	Hmm, if you hold it upside down they all seem to be languishing most charmingly on piles of jauntily arranged furniture and possessions. Where is Turkeytown, can we go there?
uncle	Sorry son it's too far. It's a land without borders in heartiest Afrique
gengis	What a golden land. Do you think they'd like to buy something?
uncle	It's possible, but we must move swiftly. The quake was followed immmediately by a terrible civil war
gengis	Heavens! We must help them!
uncle	Then a famine

gengis	Lord have mercy!
uncle	Then a surge of their national debt
gengis	Christ have mercy!
uncle	And a plunge in their credit profile
gengis	Lord have mercy! What shall we do?
uncle	Put your clothes in a brown bag and we'll mail them with a press release
gengis	Marvellous idea. I get it; the first one free, the rest they pay for
uncle	That's it
gengis	(STRIPPING)Hmm I feel good. I feel excellent. Now I'm bored. I'd like to go and exhibit myself
uncle	A trip to the theatre. I'll book tickets at once (PHONE)Hello Wally? What's on? ------Hmm "loins" a challenging exposé of a decade's housing policy, a thought provoking musical
gengis	I like it
uncle	Or, a radical reworking of the bard's great tragedy "Omlette - You can't make one without breaking eggs"
gengis	I like it better
uncle	25 tickets please, yes. We'll have a row to ourselves
gengis	Goody, we can crawl along the seats to each other waggling our tongues like this (WAGGLES HIS TONGUE)
uncle	Excellent boy!
gengis	All I want is my fingers around the greasy pole
uncle	And then?
gengis	Work it gently to see what I can get out of it like the other members of my parliament
uncle	What if nothing is forthcoming?
gengis	Then I shall take to the streets in protest
uncle	It's almost unprecedented for a head of state to get involved in demonstrations
gengis	I shall have the army with me of course

uncle	It may just swing opinion your way. There is a lady to see you
gengis	I must strip search her at once (PULLS ON RUBBER GLOVES AND A WPC HELMET)
aunty	Gengis darling!
gengis	Aunty it's you
aunty	May I have a little word?
gengis	Of course, what is it?
aunty	Well you see, you know how I love art, you know how I've always had loads of friends who are very clever and one lovely girl called Janet-with-crabs?
gengis	Yes, that well known working girl
aunty	Well we've made a little experiment with my doggie's doodoos
gengis	Yes
aunty	We've made a weally weally big pile of it and made it all dry in the sun
gengis	That's lovely aunty
aunty	And now it's as big as a house
gengis	Wow
aunty	And well, Janet-with-crabs and I thought the little people who live in the horrid smelly bit of town would like it in their little smelly park, because they love their doggies too and they also love their doggies' doodoos, I know they do because they spread it everywhere, even outside the food shops, they love their little doggies they do
gengis	Yes
aunty	And you know how Janet-with-crabs is such a friend of the people and all her work is done to help them because you know she is people too you know she told me and she used to talk like this eeow eeorw eeow (A STRONG LONDON DRAWL)
gengis	Did she?
aunty	Yes and now although she talks like us now she's still like that

	inside, she said so, even though of course she's not really because she likes all the things I like, we're like twins
gengis	Yes
aunty	Well we took the big big pile of doggie doos and put it in their tiny tiny park and the nasty scum are so thick they said it was a nasty pile of doggie doos and take it away they said, take it away and they said Janet-with-crabs, Janet-with-crabs all the time over and over and I cwied!
gengis	Well aunty, they are too stupid. Your pile of doggie doos is wasted on them
aunty	That's what I said, I said to Janet-with-crabs lets bring it here to Gengis and put it in his front room or in his garden or in his little lovely pretty park in the lovely northern suburb of H........ where he lives because he is king
gengis	No fucking way! What do I want a pile of dog shit here for, I've got enough with that little crap machine you pull around on a lead leaving its disgusting mess everywhere. My Samarkand calf slippers are ruined. Now fuck off
uncle	There is a rude man to see you oh great philosopher king
gengis	Send him -
uncle	O mighty wordsmith of the soul
gengis	Send him -
uncle	O illustrious moral engineer, jack of all trades
gengis	Send him my regards but I have a lunch appointment
uncle	He is most importunate
gengis	I am sorry for him
uncle	He is the very picture of frailty
gengis	Give him a -
uncle	He's idle, he's poor, he has everything
gengis	I'm running a fever, my clothes are sticking to me
uncle	He is most spectacularly downtrodden

gengis	He is a dreadful bore, send him away
uncle	My lord he is green with envy
gengis	Is he?
uncle	Glowing like an emerald
gengis	Poor man send him in
uncle	This way dog and make it snappy
man	Good afternoon O dainty one
gengis	You have made a horrible smear on my lino, you are much to blame. Now quickly, you have a suit for us?
man	The people have sent me to say this to you; we are all slaves -
gengis	Stop right there. I will have no such ignoble word used inside these walls.
man	Then we are the vilest... servants.. kicked like dogs -
gengis	Have some self respect man, don't affront my ears with such filth
man	What shall I say?
gengis	Don't say slaves or vile servants. Say you are journeymen. Stand upright, start again
man	We are journeymen -
gengis	Wait. I think apprentice is better
uncle	Start again
man	My Lord, the people have sent me to say we are apprentices -
gengis	Stop again. I think apprentices has a bad odour. Doesn't it put you in mind of a horrible hierachy of status. Let him say 'we are master craftsmen'
uncle	Say master craftsmen
gengis	Sorry, let him say guildsmen
man	My Lord we are guildsmen -
gengis	Good I am pleased
man	- and our children are starving, we are beaten daily and our old folk are thrown into the streets, our cripples are made laughing stocks

and our idiots are molested in all manner of ways by everyone. We languish in degradation and confusion, we are less than brutes, less than savages, we are like the quickening flies on a dung heap

gengis	Don't say cripple,say Sedate
man	Sedate my liege lord?
gengis	Yes, not lissom or agile perhaps, not acrobatic and frantic in the way of the younger healthier guildsmen, but still sedate
man	I -
gengis	For remember;I may be a spastic in my head but my body glistens from tip to prick
uncle	Un bon mot, mon petit!
gengis	Do I complain? Do I use ill-sounding words to slander my brothers? Do I use the words of a pink nose brown shorted blue shirt red neck dupe? No. I have put my house in order. I suggest that you do the same, before you prejudge, predetermine and interfere with your brothers and sisters. I think you understand me, we'll none of it
man	No My Lord
gengis	Now, was there anything else?
man	Yes, I wondered if Your Majesty required une fille à champagne?
gengis	A what?
man	Une cocotte au compot
gengis	Eh?
man	A tart My Lord, my daughter
gengis	Ah yes, send her in
man	At once O Mighty One
	GOES
gengis	Nice fella. A bit thick. And, if I'm not mistaken, a spic, a greaseball, a wop and a dago. Stank the place out. Time for the royal bath

★   ★   ★

gengis	Aunty and uncle... Why?
aunty	Because we love you

gengis	I do want a companion
uncle	A girlie?
gengis	Yes
uncle	What about the prime minister?
gengis	Too early a riser to satisfy me
aunty	(THRILLING AT HIS WORDS)We're winning, we're winning, we're winning the battle against loneliness. Can you lend me the price of a cuppa?
gengis	Wait, where are my ambassadors?
uncle	They're on their ways
aunty	They have jet lag and are sleeping it off
uncle	How shall we amuse ourselves until their return?
gengis	Perhaps I can meet the executioner?
uncle	He's busy just now. Here, read this
gengis	What is it? Hmmm, hmm, interesting!
uncle	(SNATCHES IT BACK)Give it back, not that, this
gengis	Oh
uncle	Go on,read
gengis	I can't, it's all...
uncle	Yes?
gengis	It's
uncle	Well?
gengis	Mamman told me never to
aunty	Shall we dance, I've brought my spinning top, it whistles the fandango
gengis	Doesn't it know any proper tunes?
uncle	Like what? Like the pasa double I suppose, like the old rhumbaba
gengis	I know let's rape uncle
aunty	Good boy, that's more like it. I must say, I was beginning to think you were a bit of a poof

THEY SIEZE UNCLE AND FORCE HER INTO THE BENDING OVER POSITION FROM THERE LIFTING UP UNCLE'S RAINCOAT THE GREAT KHAN GOES ABOUT HIS BUSINESS, BUT AFTER A FEW MOMENTS HE STOPS SHORT

gengis	Hmm this is not buggery as I knew it. Uncle is a woman
aunty	That's right, but your little aunty is a man. Take me I'm yours
gengis	You're not yours to give away like that. As regent I insist that you save yourself, have some modesty. This is a kingdom of losers,I want winners. The world will beg for our favours
uncle	(ADJUSTING HIS VEST)We must be patient
gengis	We'll enchant them. Death to the collaborators. Death to the traitors. Death to everyone!
aunty	Darling
gengis	Yes?
aunty	There are rumours of a plot against you
gengis	What boldness. Who would be so cruel?
aunty & uncle	It's definately no-one WE know
gengis	What happens if they succeed?
aunty & uncle	All that has been gained will be lost.
together	All that has been lost will be gained
gengis	How can we refuse?
uncle	Politely at first
gengis	And if they persist?
uncle	Then we'll expose them to the people for the overdressed fascist goons they really are
gengis	What if my people are attracted by their gaudy effects? You know what pigs they are,living in squalour and ignorance. What if they made demands on the royal purse?
uncle	We shall be ironic with them
gengis	Excellent! What if they are ironic back?
uncle	Then we shall be sarcastic
gengis	Good. And if they are sarcastic too?

uncle	Then we shall become absurd
gengis	But -
uncle	Yes?
gengis	What if they are absurd back?
uncle	Then we shall be sexy
gengis	Sexy? You mean kiss them?
uncle	Perhaps
gengis	On the lips? Is that what they call democracy?
uncle	Yes(crosses himself)
gengis	But they eat tinned fish, don't they? They smell like a cat's fart
uncle	We must try to be nimble. We must love them. As they love us
gengis	But uncle, they love me most don't they?
uncle	They idolise you
gengis	Then it's me they'll want to kiss, who knows, maybe more? You know what a kiss can lead to, you know what a vast population we have
uncle	Erm. alas no more
gengis	No?
uncle	No. There was a little accident. Most of them died
gengis	Oh. How many left?
uncle	Oh loads. Enough anyway to please Your Majesty
aunty	Oh definately
uncle	But not enough to leave you ragged
aunty	..no,no not enough for that
gengis	Well, that's a relief. You know, Aunty, Uncle, I'm beginning to feel a great warmth welling up, an affection for myself that wasn't there before. I realise that I am the focus of people's hopes and dreams and that through me many destinies will rise or fall; if I block the roads and torch the harvest, millions will suffer
uncle	Several will certainly be very upset indeed

gengis	Alright, what's next?
uncle	Dickwits, the poet laureate is rustling his leaves outside Your Majesty
gengis	At last some uplift after the drudgery of affairs of state. Drag him in

DICKWITS IS THROWN ONTO THE STAGE

dickwits	A poem Sire on the occassion of our nation's umpteenth birthday
gengis	Good, fire away
dickwits	I would like first to say a few words about the nature of poetry, the dialectic between culture and society, between society and the economy, the economy and its corollary, between the corollary and the anomally, the anomally and its astrognomy, physiognomy and ignominy, ignominy and chim-chiminy, chim-chiminy and tyranny, tyranny and-
gengis	Get on with it
dickwits	Where to start, where to start indeed. We started I think appositely in a bus shelter in Hammersmith where we were able to encourage the twenty drivers and conductors -
gengis	The poem man!
dickwits	Why do we suffer so
	I don't know
gengis	Very neat. Is there more? It's a little flat
dickwits	Oh it twists and it turns
gengis	Twist away
dickwits	I think I know, said a boy
	Said a boy
gengis	Mm
dickwits	A change of pace there
gengis	Is it likely to change again, I'm getting lost
dickwits	I think I know said a boy
	It's our master's fault

gengis	What nonsense! I demand a rewrite
dickwits	That's only the first draft. I have something else already going around in my head. It goes instead like this;

> I think I know said a boy
>
> It's somebody else's fault

gengis	That's better. But it's dull
dickwits	Dull? I think you will find that it makes people sit up straight when they hear it
gengis	If I want someone to sit up straight I'll put a railing up their arse
dickwits	Of course Your Majesty
gengis	And not before
dickwits	Quite
gengis	Aunty, tell me if I'm wrong but the poetry in this nation is lard dripping from an old man's chin on a Sunday afternoon after his dinner
aunty	Of course Your Majesty is correct
gengis	It's dreary piss on a wall. It's the splatter of shit from a fat nurse's bum who eats but cannot digest. All over the toilet bowl, then she neatly wipes it away because she's embarrassed
aunty	Your analysis is unfaltering
gengis	But she can't reach all of it
aunty	Yes!
gengis	Then she glares at you when she meets you on the communal stairway as if you've done her an injury, just because your shoes are muddy
uncle	I know the type
gengis	And leaving clay on the hallway carpet that's no more than a piece of card to hide the boards
aunty	Oh yes indeed!
gengis	The boards that are probably stained with her liquid shit, and she hates you because you see it and she's Miss fucking prim and proper

aunty	Holier than thou
uncle	Nose in the air
gengis	Smug and viscious, peeping from behind her curtain "look at him, look at her" but she's worse than the whole blooming lot of them
uncle	Squatting over her dinner plate on the floor to try to give it some flavour
aunty	Some bloody hopes
gengis	No bloody chance of that
aunty	Bloody snob
uncle	Miss Perfect
gengis	The tightest bloody fanny in Finsbury Park
	PAUSE. HE MUSES
	Sad actually, and that's art in this bloody country
uncle	You see how it upsets him. What are you going to do about it?
dickwits	I shall.. involve the community
gengis	The what??? You nincompoop. I will not have the royal poet crawling to a selection of brewers belches. And another thing;
	TENSE EXPECTATION
	These bus drivers. Louts. And they don't give a tinker's casserole for your poetry. What they want is dancing, and dancing is what you shall provide. Aunty, supply the laureate with bells and let him get on with it
uncle	Come on you, out of it
gengis	How I enjoy a debate. I told him I think didn't I?
aunty	You have singlehandedly revolutionised the written word. Would you like us to -
gengis	No, he may want to buy something
uncle	There is a superfluity of bastards in the realm Sire
gengis	And none more superfluous than Dickwits
uncle	No My Lord, little babies growing up without that most ceremo-

nious of blessings, a loving father

gengis	Gads, we must find these loving fathers and reunite them
uncle	They have buggered orf Sire
gengis	And left the little babbies? Swines. Let them stay away I say, better off without them
uncle	There is the little matter of the expense Sire, falling on the state
gengis	Expense? Scandalous. Chop off their heads!
uncle	The bastards My Lord?
gengis	Bastards louts sluts, all just baggage
uncle	Shouldn't we try to force the little families to stay together in their little hovels where they belong?
gengis	That's it, Home Sweet Home, by God in my day we stuck it out, kitchen knives, fingers in plug sockets, suicide pills, ambulance, police whatever it took
uncle	I shall tell them O great king
gengis	Tell who?
uncle	The congregation of 257 sluts with babies that is gathered by the royal drawbridge. They claim you are the father
gengis	That's impossible. Tell them I am promised to another. I'm sorry but I have a mortgage to think about. And it wasn't me
uncle	They each claim knowledge of a mole on your left buttock
gengis	There, proof! If I were the father I would hardly have had my back to them, now would I?
uncle	I shall tell them
gengis	And lest they say I am neglectful of a man's duties tell them I shall build a monument to our passions in the shape of a great tower
uncle	Marvellous idea. And what shall this edifice be called?
gengis	Borstal

★   ★   ★

uncle	The refugees from Turkeytown have arrived Your Reverence

gengis	Ok, throw them on the heap
uncle	At once. They told me to pass on their thanks in advance for the jobs
gengis	Ha ha ha
uncle	And the nice homes
gengis	He he he
uncle	Which they say are in such short supply in the war torn desert they come from
gengis	Uncle, I have noticed that the people from this particular part of Turkeytown are unusually unattractive
uncle	Yes Your Majesty
gengis	Why is that?
uncle	This flank of Turkeytown is famous for its inbreeding
gengis	I see. You know what they need in my opinion, in order to make them beautiful like us?
uncle	Yes?
gengis	Immigration
uncle	I shall arrange it immediately. Shall I round up the scum from the tower blocks and send them? Then these fellows can have their homes
gengis	No, if we move them all at once the buildings might fall down
uncle	What a shame. The Turkeytowners would have so enjoyed the terrific views
gengis	No, send the tarts who lounge around in the city hotels with their snotty children at government expense, it will save more money
uncle	And where will we put our exotic friends from the plains of Turkeytown with their multicloured blankets and their handmade folk sandals?
gengis	We shall put them in the hotels
uncle	Brilliant
gengis	You see something tells me they will enjoy the fluorescent lighting

in the bedrooms. The modernity of it will impress them. I can see it now, their children's dark little faces pressed up against the cheap double glazing marvelling at the well ordered business of our streets

uncle	Ah yes, that reminds me, a study has revealed they have no toys, the little loves
aunty	Aah what a shame!
gengis	Then send them my broken plastic launching rockets that aunty has trodden on. Give their imaginations something to dwell on
uncle	I think they're going to be very happy here. Wait till I get them to school, I have a brilliant plan
gengis	Oh yes, they will start off by singing Humpty Dumpty I hope, it's my favourite
uncle	No, no sire, not that. You see they wont be able to speak English.
gengis	Then we shall get them to sing to us in Turkeytownese
uncle	No, unfortunately they won't have mastered that either
gengis	Surely that is the language their mummies speak to them
uncle	No, no, Sire, they speak to them in English
gengis	Oh, good.
uncle	Not SO good
gengis	Why?
uncle	Because their mummies cant speak English
gengis	Then these poor infants will have no language at all
uncle	They will have two broken languages, the advantage being that they are unable to form thoughts in their heads, which makes them perfect material for our education system
gengis	Aha! I see, we shall mould them right from the start. Imbue them with the culture of their new country
uncle	Oh no Sire that would be horrid! Humpty Dumpty may be alright for you and me, and for any royal children God may grace you with (BOWS GRACEFULLY) but it is entirely unsuitable for this crew.

gengis	Oh, why?
uncle	Its English. They are foreign. It will make them feel inferior
gengis	Naturally
uncle	It's our worst fear
gengis	What about God then? and Jesus, you know how he wants them for a sunbeam
uncle	God and Jesus are English I'm afraid. These foreigners wouldn't grasp it. And then there's the embarassment of the anomalous idea of dark skinned little chaps being... sunbeams. It doesn't go does it
gengis	I suppose not
uncle	Best not to mention it
gengis	What shall we teach them then?
uncle	We shall teach them their own culture
gengis	But we don't know anything about it
uncle	Precisely, so we shall make a mish mash of foreign cultures and teach that. It will be entirely neutral, the kiddies won't notice a thing, it will wash over them leaving them.. well, numb in a painless sort of a way
gengis	What about our own little sunbeams?
uncle	You mean the white trash from the estates? They will be relieved of the terrible burden of identity and be left just as confused as the little Turkeytowners. They'll all be in the same boat
gengis	Sounds like a recipe for harmony
uncle	I like to think so

★   ★   ★

UNCLE AND AUNTY PULLING THE KHAN IN A TROIKA

gengis	Who do you think loves the people most, you and aunty, or me?
uncle	We love them in different ways
gengis	Tell me about the way you love them uncle
uncle	I love them because I know them, I share their toils and their burdens

gengis	I love them because I don't know them and don't share their toils and their burdens
uncle	I love them because they have a wise nobility
gengis	I love them because they don't
uncle	I love them because they are generous
gengis	I love them because I am generous
uncle	I love them because they are like abandoned children
gengis	I love them because I have abandoned them
uncle	I love them-
gengis	And I abandoned them because they are so ugly
uncle	I love them because through my love they will grow in body and mind and spirit
gengis	I love them because they will always remain the pigs that they are
uncle	I love them because one day they will be like me
gengis	I love them in case one day I should become like them
uncle	I love them and one day they will say to me "guide us, show us the way towards the light of universal well-being"
gengis	I love them and one day they roll me in the gutter I will look up at their contorted faces and say, "so this is how you repay my love, you dogs"
uncle	I -
gengis	"How I've suffered for you, how vile and ridiculous I have made myself on your behalfs. Have I not suffered the opprobrium of making your viscious wretched voice my own. Have I not built glorious imperial towers out of your baseness so high and exalted you have no chance of seeing them, you squinting low-life barenosed scum? Have I not rubbed my hands in your smell and said to the assembled royal banquet "smell this you toffee nosed, half arsed moneygrubbing hypocrites" Have I not as king stood on the table and lifted my skirts and shown myself to the most respected princes and queens out of utter contempt FOR THE WAITERS? Am I not a parvenu, johnnycomelately bacon chewing tyrant all so

that on this day, in this your gutter, in this cesspit of yours I could look up at your raised hobnail and say "go on stamp you monsters, but you'd be just like me if you had the balls and the brains and the great love for you all that I have!"

uncle	And what would they respond?
gengis	They'd take my wallet, and lets be fair, it would be their right
uncle	Your generosity is truly regal
gengis	They'd have a right to my wallet because it would be empty, and an empty wallet belongs to everyman. And how do you love them Aunty?
aunty	I cannot love them because they, sadly, are not worthy my love, but I do fear them, I do admire them, I do... want them
gengis	And what do you want them for Aunty?
aunty	I want them for so many things. There is a nice girlie brushes my hair and cuts my nails, and a big big man who mends my doggie when she falls over and a tiny tiny woman who clears my toilet when it blocks and they are all three so delicious I could eat them and where would I be without them... but they are not us are they, and we are not them because they beat their children and make their wives do the washing up and say all the wrong things whereas we are nice
gengis	Aunty has a point, our people are not nice, they are greedy and mean
aunty	They think only of money, they are racists sexists and imperialists
gengis	Yes, where do they get it all from?
	PAUSE FOR THOUGHT
uncle	If there's one thing I cant stand it's intolerance
aunty	Don't say that word
gengis	Intolerance?
aunty	I shall scream
gengis	You're right aunty, we shall only permit harmony. We shall say to them, live as equals, give what little you have to your brother in

need, and he shall be very grateful however small the gift, just as he is grateful for the little we give. If a man comes to you from afar speaking a strange tongue and is in need for he is an eternal pilgrim to our state for his own nation has for centuries been plundered and pillaged, then give him your home, be it ever so small and ramshackle and damp and cheaply built and horrible and ugly, for this man is in need and cannot afford anything better. For you will see in this that you have much in common. And if another man comes to your slum and says behold I am without a home, then give him your son's home or your daughter's home be they ever so humble and windswept and destitute of natural beauty except for the cheer you have brought to it with what's left of your contemptible dying out culture of cockles and mussels and inferior brands. Give this I say to your brother and though it may fall apart in his hands because it is not what he wants or deserves it is nevertheless more than you deserve; and do it not with sour words or fallen countenance, but with the correct words and bright smiles, for be warned that if you do not do it to the utmost, even though your joys are so depleted that you have nothing left to give except that which you no longer possess, if, I say, you do not do this, then it will be said that you are evil and the enemy of mankind

uncle	Quite right
gengis	I know what I should say if one of these foreign tongued johnnies came to my door asking for my big house
uncle	What is that O mighty regent?
gengis	Piss off back to the slum you come from
uncle	Of course
gengis	And if he didn't and insisted on taking up residence, I should move
uncle	Quite right
gengis	I can't live in an area full of people like that. I might be mugged or raped and you can't get real coffee
uncle	It's all just a matter of taste. We don't like ghettoes and slums
aunty	Some do, some don't

gengis	And quite apart from the poor foreign johnnies, who'd want to live next door to a load of rascist, sexist, imperialists
all three	Not us

PART II

uncle	Your majesty I have been watching the progress of the royal policy
gengis	Which one?
uncle	That of equity for all, fairness, lies, deceit, the abolition of words and a lot of money for your majesty
gengis	Yes
uncle	And I have observed its absolute success
gengis	Are my people happy?
uncle	There is a rosy glow about them to be sure (ASIDE) on their little bottoms
gengis	Good. Then it is time for phase two
uncle	What is that?
gengis	A lock out, a block out, an eclipse of the sun and moon, drown their pets, bring me their women
uncle	Most prudent
gengis	Uncle
uncle	Yes Matty
gengis	Who are these people.. My Subjects
uncle	A most unworthy bunch. One of them is a dentist, several million do nothing at all. Another is a kind of... housing officer
gengis	...Hmm that last one, bring her to me
uncle	She cannot be moved. The whole economy would grind to a halt
gengis	Then we shall go to her. Where does she live?
uncle	In the house Your Majesty
gengis	THE house. Is there but one?

uncle	For the moment sire. Building is underway
gengis	But where do the rest of my people live?
uncle	In YOUR house gracious lord
gengis	What if I want to sell?
uncle	Eviction is a top priority. Eviction and cleanliness make a nation great
gengis	Let them all appear before me then
uncle	They are... a little shy
gengis	Surely in a group they feel confident.
uncle	They are shy and.... a little ill
gengis	How ill?
uncle	Some poor souls are limbless, some headless, some bodiless
gengis	What bold disease has wrecked my population
uncle	The disease of being too cocky by half, AND not knowing the answer to a few simple questions
gengis	Is there no cure?
uncle	We sent a team of... doctors in
gengis	The result?
uncle	We're still counting
gengis	Well are there any hands or feet that you could bring me I must remain on familiar terms with my people you know
uncle	I will have aunty bring a bag at once
gengis	Good. This state business has given me an appetite - please fart into my mouth
uncle	(DOES SO)

★   ★   ★

gengis	Steady me aunty, the inspiration is upon me again; I shall grant freedoms never before dreamt of. I shall make everything illegal
aunty	The opposition your majesty..
gengis	Don't mention them. They have no poetry in their souls, no

philosophy, their arguments are based on a dilated fundament, they sit down too long in the draught and now they blame me. Withdraw their prescriptions!

aunty	Quick your majesty, a decree!
gengis	Open the prisons!
aunty	Your Majesty?
gengis	Close the prisons
aunty	?
gengis	Open them. Close them. Open them. Close them. Who can tell which is which
uncle	That is a paradox young master
gengis	No, its a dilemma, but not for me. My words come and go with the wind
aunty	What a genius. His words have no meaning whatsoever
gengis	Oppress the Lowly! Liberate the unloved
aunty	Frightening scansion!
gengis	What's bad is good, what's good is merely useful, green belt is red tape, red tape is blue ribband.... Aunty you are distant today, perhaps it is time once more for the royal bath
	SOUND OF A BATH BEING RUN
	Come on muckers who will join me?
	(THEY STRIP)
	Uncle what is that legal document in your trousers?
uncle	Oh it's nothing, merely wrapping for my member
gengis	Please let me see it, take it out
uncle	I couldn't
gengis	I can see the writing on it from here. Whose names are they? Not your conquests surely
uncle	O great king I can conceal it no longer. It is indeed a testimony of loves bourne towards me, not conquests though but subjects

gengis	My subjects?
uncle	It is a petition
gengis	It has a formidable length
uncle	They say I should snatch the crown from your head, they say the abuses of your regime are.... so many they have forgotten them
gengis	All of them? Ungrateful wretches! What must a king do?
uncle	...so I drew up a list of them myself
gengis	Ah?
uncle	They are as follows; you have usurped the role of tyrant which properly belongs to...
gengis	Who's he?
uncle	Nobody knows. You have spoken only the truth and forbidden fibbing in your cabinet
gengis	True
uncle	You have forbidden the use of paper. You have fed and clothed the hypocrite and abolished dishonesty
gengis	Thankyou. I was wondering if anyone had noticed that
uncle	You have bragged of your weakness in a most ironical tone
gengis	They cheered me for it too God bless 'em
uncle	You have pissed on the beach
gengis	It pissed on me
uncle	Industry has suffered; 100% employment, 1000% productivity, Sales nil
gengis	National pride if you'll pardon me uncle. The workers love me for it and I love them
uncle	You have housed the homeless
gengis	What statesman could do less
uncle	In a giant slum
gengis	In my own favourite city, in my own arrondisement, in my own house

uncle	And charged them exhorbitant rents
gengis	(SMILES TO HIMSELF)
uncle	And in a swingeing piece of legislative villainy that humiliated the rich and disenfranchised the poor -
gengis	Ah the double edged sword!
uncle	- You taxed all mention of the underprivaleged
gengis	What a great burden was thereby lifted from the national vocabulary. A most revealing piece of statecraft
uncle	So, with the opposition now withdrawn into self imposed exile of silence in the capital's northern suburb of H........ you empowered the bootless herd with the right of requisition creating unprecedented shifts of population and a reversal of political alliegances
aunty	He is an evil genius
uncle	You see sire, they have sinned, you have sinned, we have sinned, I, ...well I have corrected sin from my blackened soul and am now pure
gengis	Forget that now, I have something important to say to my people. (GOES TO HIS BALCONY RETURNS) I shall tell them; Lords ladies and gentlemen, forgive yourselves, forgive your brothers and sisters, forgive me, try not... try.. have faith. Don't you think that is rather moving?
uncle	Yes it is moving. But I would like to move them in some other way. (HE MANIPULATES HIS ROLLED PETITION WITH BARELY CONTROLLED FEROCITY) EXIT
gengis	Aunty, I am afraid. The kingdom once reknowned for its modest charms has become a bunker where people perform deeds of darkness upon one another
aunty	Oh its only their way
gengis	Their way of what?
aunty	Their way of saying (WITH GREAT SENTIMENTALITY) "we are people too you know"

180

gengis	Oh I see, and the murdering and torturing that goes on in our parks and woodlands for entertainment?
aunty	Oh its only their little way
gengis	Their little way of what?
aunty	Their little way of saying "sometimes we're lonely, sometimes we're afraid, sometimes we don't really know what is wrong; so we take someone and we pull their teeth out with pliers, then set fire to them, a little group of chums together, girls and boys, supportive, caring,no nasty words"
gengis	What does it all mean aunty?
aunty	(FEROCIOUS) It means the devil is amongst us, put the boot in hard while you've still got the chance. Put bars up at your window, don't talk to yourself after 8pm, don't give an inch or they'll take a mile, string em up, cut them down. You see?
gengis	Yes, I see
aunty	It's just their little way of saying (BABY TALK) We're lost and lost and lost and lost and we don't know our way home. (MORE SO) We want some more money.
gengis	But wait. I want some more money
aunty	Don't interrupt. It's their little way of saying, we want free this free that and free the other
gengis	Bastards! Wait till I catch them
aunty	They want you to be their scape goat
gengis	Do they?
aunty	They want to blame you for the piss in their lifts
gengis	But I'm a socialist. I would never piss in a lift
aunty	Perhaps you haven't explained that well enough. You must communicate
gengis	I'll make a play a book a poem
aunty	That way they'll all understand. They love plays and books and poems

gengis	But how? They're all so thick
aunty	We'll put it on television and call it Bingo Wingo Zingo Zam Powee
gengis	What if they come round to watch it on my tv set? I'm not having any of them in here, they all stink of air freshener. Do they wear toilet cleaner as perfume?
aunty	Yes son they do
gengis	Maybe it's too late to help them
aunty	Aaah don't say that. Imagine their little faces looking up at you with their big eyes "please help us don't to be such ignorant Tory Goons"
gengis	The bigoted swines. The thought of them makes me want not just to piss in their lifts but to shit on their brains
aunty	It's been done. They have done it to themselves. Out of sheer bloody-mindedness of course
gengis	Ha! So British. So land of hope and glory. So UK
aunty	Doesn't it make you proud to be not British
gengis	Yes, urgh! I'm half Maltese
aunty	I'm half Madagascan
gengis	I'm half Chinese
aunty	I'm half Indonesian
gengis	I'm half Polynesian
aunty	I'm half Melanesian
gengis	I'm half MALVENIAN
aunty	I'm supporting the African teams in the World cup
gengis	I'm supporting India in the alternative World cup
aunty	I'm supporting rabbits in the animal World cup
gengis	I'm supporting poor little pussies in the World Cup for animals with electrodes in their little brains
aunty	I'm supporting animals that aren't in any teams because they are too sick because they've been eaten by doggies in the garden

gengis	YOU HIPPOCRITE!
aunty	?
gengis	You train your dog to kill the very birds in the trees
aunty	Only Bedause he's hungwy…
gengis	Remind me, what is it just their little way of saying?
aunty	It's just thier little way of saying that when the suffering is all too much it's time to stop for a few moments of reflection, a little sadness fills your heart, you can't go on, a tear comes to your eye, a sob mounts inside your head chest throat your eye, your vision blackens, a whisper from far away says "someone, please if there is anyone, please forgive us"
gengis	But aunty why don't we all love each other anymore? Has it always been like this?
aunty	I hope you don't think I'm old enough to remember?
gengis	Sometimes I get so depressed aunty
aunty	What you need is something to cheer you up
gengis	I know! The assizes! Justice!
aunty	That's right. It'll put the colour back in your cheeks
gengis	Bring in the first accused
aunty	The first accused is… Dickwits
	DICKWITS IS THROWN ONTO THE STAGE
gengis	Ah Dickwits, you bastard. What have you done to my people? You have ravaged them haven't you with your horrible claustrophobia. You've tried to hypnotise them but they didn't want you did they, they didn't fancy it. Well serve you right. They've turfed you out haven't they, but not before you degraded their palettes, they were gourmets once now they drink vinegar, even the babies. This is all down to your moral rectitude which you keep inviting everyone to examine. Well you've bent over once too often Dickwits, you've smiled sideways at the camera for the last time, you promised so much and delivered so little, you're on your way to the awards ceremony in the sky, see what the cherubim make of your

inauguration speach and while you're at it you can cast my vote for me in the general election, then we'll see what you smell like when you're laughing on the other side of your face, counting your onions in your rotten borough. You think I don't know, you think I don't care, well look at these - real tears! Real tears mark you, not bought with your socialist shilling, not banged out on your Country Life anvil either, none of your cold steel here Charlie I can assure you, none of your street carnivals and residents committees where I come from, we didn't submit it to a panel in my comprehensive mate; playing fields? what bloomin' playing fields? Just turn the page and read on. You're plain Jane, Dicky boy, you're drab, right down to your wife's bangles and your beads and your patent leather shoes and your aerosol can. You've tidied up a bit too much is all I can say, you've hoovered my favourite tree and strangled that little Dicky bird with your endless bloody explanations. You want a goal for tomorrow, I know you do my fairweather friend, you may not recognise this court my fine fellow but we saw YOU coming a mile off so there's no use in shrugging your shoulders you're in there somewhere, by Christmas! You won't be sitting on that wall for long with this morning's egg on your face, don't worry about that, because you've been bought. Oh didn't you think you were a retail item? Retail? Retail. You're in the bloody clearance sale mate, you were NEVER full price, you can call it priceless if you want but I know what your posh customers call it on their way home behind your back. You don't know what I'm referring to do you, you don't know what I mean? It's all greek to you isn't it Charlie until you're sick of hearing it. Well, have you ever wondered why? Help me down from here, I'm ready for my operation. You perform it Dicky boy, because I know you mean well and I'm grateful. I trust you, more than I'd trust a friend. Bless you darling. Ok doctor I'm ready, get your cross-saws out.

UNCLE HAS RETURNED WITH THE NECESSARY EQUIPMENT

TREPANNING BEGINS

uncle	You see Dicky boy how you have won the royal favour? He skirted

around it now but there's no denying how your muscular verse style and poetic diction has made a deep impression on his temporal lobe. This could be your opportunity to jog his memory

DICKWITS SAWS ASSIDUOUSLEY

gengis   (SPEAKING FROM THE OPERATING TABLE) You can't hide it from me any longer, I have no kingdom left do I?

uncle   Well, no...

gengis   What darkness is this, what sadness fills the world? What have I done?

uncle   One or two misjudged policies

gengis   Tell me, wasn't I radical enough?

uncle   Radical? You have chopped down to the roots and laid them bare

aunty   The whole kingdom goes about without a stitch of clothing on its back. Not a fault is hidden

uncle   Our wounds, all our sores

aunty   ...our blisters

uncle   ...our broken limbs

aunty   ...our torn eyelids, open beside the ditches

uncle   the whole nation groans. There's no talk of a lack of radicalism

aunty   No-one says if only he were

uncle   ...more

aunty   ...radical

uncle   No-one

aunty   ...for they cannot speak

uncle   Not a man among them can utter a word

aunty   ...enough to say -

uncle   ...more radical please

aunty   No worry on that score

gengis   I don't know then...

PAUSE

	...perhaps I wasn't moderate enough
aunty	Of course you were. You have been moderate. in moderation
uncle	When it suits. Have you ever wanted to be moderate and not been
gengis	No
uncle	There then moderate with a free will
aunty	Randomly moderate with a free hand
uncle	You have dispensed moderation with liberality, with a glad hand
aunty	Generously giving it away like gifts to your friends
uncle	Here friend, aunt, uncle here is a moderate gift, a gift given in moderation
	SAWING CONTINUES, UNCLE SLIPS OUT
gengis	Aunty, what is life all about?
aunty	That, nephew, is one of life's little mysteries
gengis	When will the mystery be solved?
aunty	Just before its all over, when you will realise in the words of Dickwits here our national bard "all is vanity" In the face of death you will suddenly come over all sick and all scared and the allure of vain projects will pass away; Your books - you were never to read them, Your beautiful home - you were never to live in it, Your beautiful wife is a failure, Your favourite side of bacon in the pantry - covered in bile. It will all disappear
gengis	How do you know this aunty?
aunty	(WHISPERS TO HIM)
gengis	Is that why you so often smile secretly to yourself in that strange way?
aunty	(DOES SO) Perhaps
gengis	I am glad you have revealed these things to me aunty for I am now glad that this nation has been relieved of its its its -
aunty	Its...
gengis	..well everything
aunty	Yes

gengis	It is a good thing for the people because they are closer now to the meaning of life as revealed in the last moments of bitter painful nausia you described so well
aunty	Thankyou
gengis	Keep a nation close to death and they will be close to life
aunty	Yes, that is true. True words son. True, true words
gengis	Unfortunately I don't think my people have benefitted from the terrible knowledge available to them
aunty	Why not?
gengis	Because they are all watching TV
aunty	Bless them
gengis	What is that clumping bumping sound?
aunty	That musical marching?
gengis	Yes that clomping and stomping
aunty	That clippity cloppity?
gengis	Yes that munching and crunching
aunty	That Hippity boppity?
gengis	Yes that gnashing and grinding
aunty	That skippity hoppity?
gengis	Yes, that horrible noise!
aunty	That's your uncle on his horse
gengis	He must make a fine figure of a man. Aunty I have begun to notice a sublime look upon Uncle's face. Perhaps he has discovered this enlightenment you speak of? And just now, well it must have been an apparition...
aunty	Dreamy boy what did you see?
gengis	Uncle, in a small room with what appeared to be.... friends
aunty	One of his workshops
gengis	They were waving their arms in the air
aunty	Just a warm up dearie to prevent it all becoming too headbound

gengis	And when I asked what they were doing they turned at once and looked at me with strange hollow eyes
aunty	They were probably just tired Gengis darling, your uncle is a terrible bore when he's helping people express themselves
gengis	But aunty, there was a strange sense of evil in the room

UNCLE BURSTS IN

uncle	Yes and what's wrong with that you little squealer
gengis	But uncle you were always so loving and caring
uncle	Yes, and I shall love my people all the more once they have achieved the perfection I have planned for them
gengis	It sounds wonderful. And what kind of perfection do you have in mind?
uncle	In my dream kingdom supplicants line the streets. They fling money at you as you pass by, they lurk in every shop doorway and you are expected to hurl insults at them in return
gengis	Is it easy to think of any?
uncle	I usually cry out things like; nit-pickers! slow brains! limping fellows! ant-teasers! Operatives! rotten vest!
gengis	Are they pleased with these?
uncle	I mention only a few of their favourites. I shall give animus to the pusilanimous, I shall make the crooked straight, where there is doubt I shall bring certainty, I shall never surrender
gengis	How will you do all this uncle?
uncle	Words
gengis	Aha
uncle	Yes it's all a matter of finding the right words
gengis	And if that doesn't work?
uncle	Then I have this big knobbledy stick
gengis	Then you are bound to succeed. We are looking forward to the new order aren't we aunty?
aunty	Yes dear

gengis	But uncle, those strange leather boots
uncle	Inside the top of my boots I have frogs for my enemies
aunty	Urgh!
uncle	Beware the man who denies my people the right to be very happy indeed
gengis	Beware indeed
uncle	Nothing but the best for my boys
aunty	Quite right
uncle	The quest awaits me
gengis	And will you bring back food to feed the hungry babies?
uncle	Better than that. I shall return at the head of a dark-browed column of the red-trimmed sons of judgement
aunty	How thrilling and chilling
gengis	But uncle I'm afraid, I like things as they are. I like being Gengis Khan, I like being the people's choice, I like taking everyone's money uncle, I like eating my little bowl of mumsmilk yoghurt of an evening, I like cheating in the elections and tricking the people and I like reading pornography in the bath, please don't spoil it
uncle	Call that destiny, you money grubbing degenerate, you low minded sensualist pervert you? - (FARTS LOUDLY)
gengis	Uncle, you have farted
uncle	Yes and let that be a warning to you. I shall expell all unnatural gases from the temple of my rectum until the whole of europe stinks of my evacuation. I shall be free and you my lad will cough your Jewish lungs onto the table. (DOES SO)
gengis	Does this mean no World Cup?
uncle	There will be one but my team will win or several million will live to regret it
	THE DOG BARKS AT HIM
	Tell that thing to shut up
aunty	I can't sweetie he's excited by the noisome cloud still clinging to your slacks

uncle	Then I shall silence his indignity. (HE STAMPS ON THE PUPPY'S NECK RENDERING IT SILENT)
aunty	Oh brute, brute, poor little doggie! You wicked man, you cruel man!
	UNCLE MARCHES OUT
aunty	What a terrible change. Do you think we should have his throat cut to preserve world peace?
gengis	No, he may want to buy something
aunty	Sing us some gentle songs of suffering
gengis	I've trained long and hard for this. Quick tie me up, lower me down, into the royal casket, this is no headcold. Don't you recognise the imperial goitre when you see it?
aunty	Uncle! the razor sharp incisions of our national poet have finally brought the tyrant to his last breath. Come back quick!
uncle	(ENTERS) Incredible. But shall the nation be denied one last good-bye?
gengis	Alright, file them past but make it quick, the royal memories are washing over my conciousness. Gee whizz uncle, I was truely a pippin!
uncle	Bien sûr
gengis	Who are these people aunty?
aunty	They are your subjects
gengis	O their breaths are certainly no sweeter than when I came to the throne. Has it really all been in vain? Fuck damn my own stupid head for thinking up this idea, but I'll stick to it anyway. It will improve, where is Dickwits?
dickwits	I'm sorry Your Highness, you were trepanned in good faith
gengis	What part of my brain did they remove?
dickwits	Your judgement Sire. And you'll find your backhand in tennis a good deal worse
gengis	My way with women is intact I see

(A WORTHY ERECTION PROTRUDES THE BLANKET)

dickwits	Ah the hangmans cudgel, as we call it Your Majesty
gengis	Dicky, forgive me if I have been glib with you. I love you
dickwits	You're fading fast Your Majesty. Should I pen a dying speech for you, your last words?
gengis	Not on your life Dicky boy, even a farting corpse is more eloquent than the squeaking of your pips. Thanks but no thanks

DICKWITS BOWS AND EXITS BACKWARDS

gengis	You wait. Indira will come back one day and you'll see. All this piffle-paffle, all this... politics! Indira is beautiful, Indira is full of love, Indira has a temple of humanity in her breast, Indira has long black hair and smoothe feet, and they are walking this way I can sense it
aunty	And what do you think she'll make of you?
gengis	She loves the people and they love her, she IS the people. She is me. I am her. I am the people. I love her. I love the people. I love myself
uncle	It's all very well to come out with all this now I must say. We haven't noticed you being very loving, have we?
aunty	No
uncle	We haven't noticed you kissing little babies and having a joke with the pensioners. You're not exactly an antivivisectionist are you, not exactly a vegan, not exactly a supporter of freedom fighters on the street corners on a saturday morning with a bucket and a newspaper are you?
gengis	I'm anti abortion
aunty	You papist!
gengis	Aha, so you'll like me to persecute catholics now?
uncle	NOT if they're Irish and wave the tricolour
gengis	Damned if I can keep track of it
uncle	Your frivolous attitude reduces politics to mere flibber flabber, blibby blabby, gibber gabber

gengis	It's your fault, you keep moving the goal posts
uncle	Gengis, don't worry, just do as we do, say what we say, we'll keep an eye on you
gengis	Thanks uncle. I do try
uncle	Alright good boy. His heart is in the right place
aunty	It's all over the bloody place. What he needs is a good kick in the cunt!
uncle	Alright aunty, we shall kick him there if he does it again
aunty	Hear? So just watch it
uncle	Isn't it sad to see a noble man sunk so low
aunty	And all because he tried to steal the march on his neighbour
uncle	But what a neighbour. People are saying he was not a man of total frankness regarding his relations with Indira
aunty	What treachery. So it was all a mirage
uncle	Remember how he went bankrupt soon after Indira left, and he shut up shop and disappeared? It transpires they were seen naked together on the banks of a river
aunty	And this is the sad eyed godess who so castigated poor Gengis for his little retailing peccadillo!
uncle	The very same, laughing in the moonlight with the sperm of her husband's rival swimming in her beautiful brown belly... So they say
gengis	When Indira comes I shall not ask her where she's been. Perhaps on her arrival she will give birth to the child of a fornicator and that child I shall wrap up in my arms and take it out and show my people; behold your deliverer! I shall call out to them, and they shall cry tears of joy

★   ★   ★

DAY. DAWN. NIGHT. TWIGHTLIGHT. DAY. DAWN. NIGHT. DAWN. TWIGHLIGHT. DAWN. DAY. NIGHT

gengis	Stop that

aunty	Well, what's next Plucky?
gengis	I shall merge the VD and cancer clinics. Better atmosphere and save money
uncle	Getting a little nervous about the approach of your beloved?
gengis	She loves me uncle. She loves me. She loves me. ME. She loves me. ME ME ME
uncle	If indeed she has the roving eye your days are surely numbered. You'd better get out quick in a getaway car
gengis	Will you drive in that case uncle?
uncle	Sorry son, cramp in my right hand, lassitude of my left
gengis	Aunty darling, we'll drive off together. We'll stop off and get some shopping
aunty	Can we can we can we really?
gengis	Yes alright
aunty	In my favourite mall, in my favourite shopping centre. I love the fountains, soft stream of light
gengis	That's right aunty
aunty	No fucking riff raff there
gengis	No
aunty	Just shoppers, shopping shopping shopping shopping shopping shopping shopping shopping shopping
gengis	Buying toys at christmas most of them
aunty	Yippee
gengis	Big new duvets and sideboards
aunty	Oooo
gengis	Holidays
aunty	Yippee
gengis	Watches
aunty	Watches!
gengis	Lovely shoppers aunty, all waiting for you to come and join in

aunty	Yippee
gengis	Boom and bust boom and bust
aunty	Yippee
gengis	But watch out aunty, keep your hands to yourself
aunty	Alright but if any police get in my way I'll fucking run them down
gengis	Alright, that's ok
aunty	I'll fucking go window shopping with them on the bumper
gengis	(SUDDEN TEARS) It's no good I love her, I love her, I want my baby
uncle	But she doesn't want you. Not since the days of the old shoponthecorner have you heard so much as a postcard. You see she has become interested in world affairs
gengis	What? You mean she watches the news?
uncle	Yes
gengis	Then... she's well informed
uncle	Yes
gengis	She knows what's going on?
uncle	Yes she does and she reads the newspapers listens to the radio and looks at pictures, she's plugged in, she's got your number
gengis	Bitch. I hate women like that
uncle	You can't argue with progress
gengis	They glance at Titbits and they think they're Bertolucci
uncle	I know
gengis	Ignorance is the bane of our age
	VERY LONG PAUSE
gengis	Most people are too dumb to realise that
aunty	Ready sonny?
gengis	It's no good, I can't go. Without her I am nothing
aunty	She'll chop your little head off
gengis	But first I shall taste the sweet sorrow of her rebuke,It is enough
uncle	Then you will have to watch while I supply her with all the evidence against you

gengis	Of course good kind uncle. You are a man of high ideals for which no sacrifice is too great, no treachery too low. I understand
uncle	That's correct my boy. You shall be an egg in my omelette
gengis	I shan't protest. If she says I was ambitious I shall say I am a man, if she says I was cruel, I shall say I loved only justice, if she says I was rash I shall say I am a poet at heart, if she says I was corrupt I shall say my duty has corrupted me, if she says I lied I shall say I love the truth too much to speak it, if she says I stole the lightbulbs I shall show her the palace of lights I built in her honour, if she says I betrayed my country I shall say I have no country for I am a child of the universe and anyone who believed otherwise was a sucker, if she says I betrayed my class I shall say my class has produced quite enough heroes for any epoch, if she says I betrayed my god I shall bless her, if she says I burnt books I shall show her my poems, if she says I trampled the blind and mislead the lame, well, I am no doctor and neither is she, if she says I believe in an incorrect political analysis, I shall say the analysis believes me but I believe no-one, if she says I am a tyrant I shall inform her that in the name of democracy all my policy decisions were taken by the cleaners, you'd better take it up with them, if she says I buggered aunty's doggie I shall say who can resist that sexy little pet and its waddle, and if she says I have no love I shall crash my cymbals and dance and sing and say YES! Let us speak of love!
uncle	Dickwits has made himself visible through the portcullis
gengis	What does he want?
uncle	He can't say, he's unusually short of wind
gengis	You'd better let him in or he'll say I'm playing hard to get
	DICKWITS IS THROWN ONTO THE STAGE
gengis	Well, what is it?
dickwits	The beautiful Indira is coming. She is walking across the desert at the head of a large force
gengis	At last. Where are you going uncle?
uncle	I'm going to meet her. Coming aunty?

aunty	Yes, of course. Lovely girl
gengis	It's me she wants
uncle	Ok Gengis, one last request, before Indira comes
gengis	One last request. Alright. A cigarette. No, two cigarettes. No a cigar
uncle	It has been smoked, sorry
gengis	Alright then, a meal
uncle	The doggie has just eaten it I'm afraid
gengis	Anything will do then
uncle	Anything at all?
gengis	Anything
uncle	Name something
gengis	A magazine
uncle	Neither of us can reach
gengis	Get me some money
uncle	Money?
gengis	Yes! Sell someone something
uncle	There's nothing to sell that everyone hasn't already got
gengis	Get me a merchant
uncle	He's in his yacht
gengis	Get me an architect
uncle	He's in his rectangle
gengis	Get me lions and tigers
uncle	They are printed in a book
gengis	Get me my philosopher
uncle	He's crowded in his house
gengis	Get me a museum
uncle	It's under ground
gengis	Get me a park with fountains

196

uncle	We've moved it outside town
gengis	Get me an honest man to be my friend
uncle	He's on tv
gengis	Get me a beautiful girl
uncle	She's unable
gengis	Get me a smell
uncle	It's on your fingers

DICKWITS PUTS THE NOOSE AROUND HIS KNECK

gengis	Get me a rope
uncle	It's around your neck
gengis	Get me a priest
uncle	He's singing his song and clapping his hands
gengis	Get me a blindfold
uncle	It's nowhere to be seen
gengis	Get me a tree
uncle	There's only two planks

DICKWITS HELPS HIM ONTO A CHAIR

gengis	Get me a chair
uncle	You're on it
gengis	Get me a pardon

UNCLE GIVES SILVER TO DICKWITS WHO EXITS

uncle	Can't hear you
gengis	Get the hangman
uncle	He's spending his guinea
gengis	Get me Indira Indira Indira!
uncle	She's right here, just coming
gengis	Aunty, why do the men and women have no forgiveness in their hearts?
aunty	Because it would burst their little hearts

gengis	Aunty, why do their eyes fill with tears?
aunty	They're thinking about the tears in their eyes like me what I do when I want to cry
gengis	Aunty why do I never win a prize?
aunty	Because there is no prize for you
gengis	Aunty why does the wind blow?
aunty	Because of those nasty weather men
gengis	Aunty, why has my tree fallen down?
aunty	I cannot tell a lie, you cut it down with your big shiny axe of silver and gold you did you cut it down
gengis	Aunty why are we out here in the terrible cold
aunty	Because we are together holding hands
gengis	Aunty, why can no-one read the book?
aunty	Upsidedowninsideoutbacktofront
gengis	Aunty, why the biggest babboon?
aunty	Because the kangaroo shoes jump higher
gengis	Aunty, why so quiet in the sky?
aunty	Because the crows are cawing elsewhere
gengis	Aunty why the ragged soldier in his trench
aunty	Because the shiny general on his horse
gengis	Why the judge upon his bench?
aunty	Because the rope around his neck
gengis	Aunty, what happens when you plant a seed?
aunty	The seed begins to grow
gengis	What happens when the seed begins to grow?
aunty	The clouds begin to fill with snow
gengis	What happens when the snow begins to fall?
aunty	The birdie sits upon the wall
gengis	What happens when the wall begins to crack?

aunty	The stick falls down upon your back
gengis	What happens when my back begins to bleed?
aunty	Then you are dead and dead indeed
gengis	What happens when the cat's away?
aunty	The mice begin to play

AUNTY TIPTOES OFF

gengis   Aunty, I'm frightened

GENGIS STANDS ON THE CHAIR WITH THE ROPE AROUND HIS NECK

END